Data Analysis Plans
A Blueprint for Success Using SAS®

Kathleen Jablonski • Mark Guagliardo

§.sas®   support.sas.com/bookstore

The correct bibliographic citation for this manual is as follows: Jablonski, Kathleen and Mark Guagliardo. 2016. *Data Analysis Plans: A Blueprint for Success Using SAS®*. Cary, NC: SAS Institute Inc.

Data Analysis Plans: A Blueprint for Success Using SAS®

Copyright © 2016, SAS Institute Inc., Cary, NC, USA

All Rights Reserved. Produced in the United States of America.

For a hard copy book: No part of this publication may be reproduced, stored in a retrieval system, or transmitted, in any form or by any means, electronic, mechanical, photocopying, or otherwise, without the prior written permission of the publisher, SAS Institute Inc.

For a web download or e-book: Your use of this publication shall be governed by the terms established by the vendor at the time you acquire this publication.

The scanning, uploading, and distribution of this book via the Internet or any other means without the permission of the publisher is illegal and punishable by law. Please purchase only authorized electronic editions and do not participate in or encourage electronic piracy of copyrighted materials. Your support of others' rights is appreciated.

U.S. Government License Rights; Restricted Rights: The Software and its documentation is commercial computer software developed at private expense and is provided with RESTRICTED RIGHTS to the United States Government. Use, duplication, or disclosure of the Software by the United States Government is subject to the license terms of this Agreement pursuant to, as applicable, FAR 12.212, DFAR 227.7202-1(a), DFAR 227.7202-3(a), and DFAR 227.7202-4, and, to the extent required under U.S. federal law, the minimum restricted rights as set out in FAR 52.227-19 (DEC 2007). If FAR 52.227-19 is applicable, this provision serves as notice under clause (c) thereof and no other notice is required to be affixed to the Software or documentation. The Government's rights in Software and documentation shall be only those set forth in this Agreement.

SAS Institute Inc., SAS Campus Drive, Cary, NC 27513-2414

August 2016

SAS® and all other SAS Institute Inc. product or service names are registered trademarks or trademarks of SAS Institute Inc. in the USA and other countries. ® indicates USA registration.

Other brand and product names are trademarks of their respective companies.

Contents

About This Book vii
About the Author xi
Acknowledgments xiii

Chapter 1 / Preface **1**
    Preface 1

Chapter 2 / Introduction **3**
    Data Analysis Plans 3

Chapter 3 / Before the Plan: Develop an Analysis Policy ... **5**
    Summary 5
    The Analysis Policy 6
    Analysis Policy Components 7
    Analysis Policies for Large Projects 11
    Example Project Analysis Policy 11
    References 14

Chapter 4 / Outline of a Plan **17**
    Summary 17
    Outline of a Typical Plan 18

Chapter 5 / The Plan Introduction **21**
    Summary 21
    Objectives, Hypotheses or Questions, and Aims 22
    Identify the Project Team 24
    Identify the Target Audience 25

Chapter 6 / Hypotheses, Questions, and Study Design ... **27**
    Summary 27
    Conceptualizing the Problem 28
    Hypotheses 29
    Research Questions 29
    Study 29
    Identifying Confounders 31
    Communicating with the Study Team 32

Chapter 7 / Data Description — 33
- Summary — 33
- Data Sources — 33
- Data Definitions — 35
- Data Summary — 36
- Reviewing the Data with the Study Team — 37

Chapter 8 / Data Exploration — 39
- Summary — 39
- Descriptive Statistics for Major Variables — 40
- Exploring Outliers and Problematic Data Distributions — 42
- Distribution Problems — 46
- Determining the Source of Variability — 49
- Producing Baseline Tables — 55
- Communicating with the Project Team — 57

Chapter 9 / Analysis — 59
- Summary — 59
- General Approach — 60
- Analysis of Questions/Hypotheses — 63
- References — 69

Chapter 10 / Potential Conclusions, Study Weaknesses, and a Timeline — 71
- Summary — 71
- Potential Conclusions — 71
- Limitations and Weaknesses — 72
- Timeline — 72

Chapter 11 / Revising, Producing and Sharing the Plan — 73
- Summary — 73
- Communicating and Revising the Plan — 73
- Turning the Plan into a Report — 74
- Developing Tabular Presentations — 74
- Cross-References — 75
- Unplanned Analysis — 75
- Closing Remarks — 76

Chapter 12 / Example Analysis Plan: The TIAD Study — 77
- Summary — 78
- Introduction — 78
- Questions — 79
- Data Description — 79

Initial Data Tables and Variable Distributions 80
General Approach 82
Analysis of Hypotheses 83

Index **87**

About This Book

Purpose

Data Analysis Plans: A Blueprint for Success Using SAS® is a getting started guide to building an effective data analysis plan with a solid foundation for planning and managing your analytics projects. Data analysis plans are critical to the success of analytics projects. When implemented effectively, they facilitate team focus and communication through a mutual understanding of goals, data, and methods. In this way, workflow is improved and client expectations are well managed. This book provides step-by-step instructions to write, implement, and update your data analysis plan. It emphasizes the concept of an analysis plan as a working document that is updated throughout the life of a project, and may evolve into a sound and comprehensive draft for a final report or publication.

Is This Book for You?

This book was written primarily for applied statisticians and data analysts in the early stages of their career, when they are building foundational knowledge for performing data analyses in a consultative role. Analysts in environments such as university research support centers, corporate or government strategic planning and analysis departments, and private endeavors such as think tanks and management consulting firms will find this book helpful. However, this book also provides more experienced SAS users with the opportunity to adjust how they plan and conduct analytic projects. For them, the book can serve as a guide for establishing more fruitful and productive relationships with collaborators and clients. Subject areas include medical research, public health research, social studies, educational testing and evaluation, and environmental studies.

Prerequisites

While a basic knowledge of SAS is assumed, SAS code and program examples are given. It is assumed that the reader has some experience with the SAS data step and SAS procedure syntax.

Scope of This Book

The book explains how analysis planning is comparable to a home construction blueprint. Just as a blueprint adheres to local building codes, an analytics support group should have analysis policies to guide all of their analysis planning. The book shows you how to develop these policies. Guidance is then provided for identifying project team players and roles, and developing clear questions or hypotheses that directly address project goals and are suitable given the available data. The ensuing chapters cover the importance of describing the data sources and fields in the shared plan, and conducting and reporting data explorations to reveal and resolve potential problems such as outliers and unsuitable data value distributions. Next, the book demonstrates how to present the analyses that are appropriate for the agreed upon questions or hypotheses. The final chapters explain why and how to document potential conclusions and study weaknesses, and how to implement the plan with the goal of turning it into final report or publication.

The book is not a primer on inferential statistical methods required for most analyses. It is assumed that the statistician or analyst has sufficient training to choose statistical methods that are appropriate for their project, and understands the mathematical assumptions required of those methods.

About the Examples

Software Used to Develop the Book's Content

SAS BASE 9.4

Example Code and Data

You can access the example code and data for this book by linking to its author page at http://support.sas.com/publishing/authors. Select the name of the author. Then, look for the cover thumbnail of this book, and select Example Code and Data to display the SAS programs that are included in this book.

If you are unable to access the code through the Web site, send e-mail to saspress@sas.com.

Using SAS® University Edition? You can download SAS® University Edition for free, directly from SAS, then use the code and data sets provided with this book. Get started by visiting http://support.sas.com/publishing/import_ue.data.html.

Additional Resources

Although this book illustrates many analyses regularly performed in businesses across industries, questions specific to your aims and issues may arise. To fully support you, SAS Institute and SAS Press offer you the following help resources:

- For questions about topics covered in this book, contact the author through SAS Press:
    - Send questions by email to saspress@sas.com; include the book title in your correspondence.
    - Submit feedback on the author's page at http://support.sas.com/author_feedback.
- For questions about topics in or beyond the scope of this book, post queries to the relevant SAS Support Communities at https://communities.sas.com/welcome.
- SAS Institute maintains a comprehensive website with up-to-date information. One page that is particularly useful to both the novice and the seasoned SAS user is its Knowledge Base. Search for relevant notes in the "Samples and SAS Notes" section of the Knowledge Base at http://support.sas.com/resources.
- Registered SAS users or their organizations can access SAS Customer Support at http://support.sas.com. Here you can pose specific questions to SAS Customer Support; under Support, click Submit a Problem. You will need to provide an email address to which replies can be sent, identify your organization, and provide a customer site number or license information. This information can be found in your SAS logs.

Keep in Touch

We look forward to hearing from you. We invite questions, comments, and concerns. If you want to contact us about a specific book, please include the book title in your correspondence.

To Contact the Author through SAS Press

By e-mail: saspress@sas.com

Via the Web: http://support.sas.com/author_feedback

SAS Books

For a complete list of books available through SAS, visit http://support.sas.com/bookstore.

Phone: 1-800-727-3228

Fax: 1-919-677-8166

E-mail: sasbook@sas.com

SAS Book Report

Receive up-to-date information about all new SAS publications via e-mail by subscribing to the SAS Book Report monthly eNewsletter. Visit http://support.sas.com/sbr.

Publish with SAS

SAS is recruiting authors! Are you interested in writing a book? Visit http://support.sas.com/saspress for more information.

About the Authors

Kathleen Jablonski Kathleen Jablonski, PhD, is an applied statistician in the Milken School of Public Health at George Washington University where she mentors students in research design and methods using SAS for data management and analysis. Her interests include study design, statistics, and epidemiology. She has served as principal investigator, as well as lead statistician, on several multicenter NIH funded studies and networks. She received a PhD in biological anthropology and a Master of Science in Applied Statistics.

Mark Guagliardo Mark Guagliardo, PhD, is an analyst with the Veterans Health Administration, U.S. Department of Veterans Affairs and has used SAS for 35 years on a wide variety of data management and analysis tasks. He has been the principal investigator or co-investigator for dozens of federally funded grants and contracts, primarily in the area of health services research. His peer reviewed publications and presentations have been in the areas of health services, public health, pediatrics, geography, and anthropology. He is a certified GIS (geographic information systems) professional, and specializes in studies of access to health care services locations.

Learn more about these authors by visiting their author pages, where you can download free book excerpts, access example code and data, read the latest reviews, get updates, and more:

http://support.sas.com/publishing/authors/jablonski.html

http://support.sas.com/publishing/authors/guagliardo.html

Acknowledgments

We dedicate this book to our parents, Bernard Jablonski and Patricia King Jablonski, and Frank Guagliardo, Jr. and Fay Ann Tycer Guagliardo, who instilled in us the foundational principle of this book: If something is worth doing, it is worth doing right the first time. We thank our daughters for their assistance. Sarah Anne J. Guagliardo counseled us on the theme and direction of the book and painted the cover art. Laura J. Guagliardo provided valuable edits and some very timely encouragement.

Thank you to our SAS Press team: Brenna Leath for developmental editing, Kathy Underwood for copyediting, Robert Harris for graphic design, Denise T. Jones for production, Cindy Puryear for marketing, and Ellen Mir and Danny Modlin for their technical review.

The first author is grateful to Dr. Mary Foulkes, Research Professor of Biostatistics and Epidemiology, The George Washington University for her continual mentoring and her support while writing this book.

Preface

Preface 1

Preface

The topic of analysis planning usually receives cursory attention in research design classes, and that may be the only exposure professional analysts ever receive. Moreover, the literature provides very little guidance. There are many one- or two-page articles about analysis plans, and a number of books on research project planning and execution allude to them. However, to our knowledge, this is the first comprehensive coverage of analysis plans.

Sometimes the data analysis plan is referred to as a statistical analysis plan. Since it is usually data that is analyzed and not statistics, we use the term data analysis plan.

This book is intended to teach data analysts how to write an analysis plan for different purposes, and how to use the analysis plan as a working document throughout the life cycle of a project. It is written for the beginning analyst but may provide insight on ways to improve and expand analysis plans for intermediate and advanced analysts.

Throughout the book, we use the term *client* to refer to the outside person or group who has initiated the research question and may be paying for your services. However, the client may be your research co-investigator, another colleague, or yourself if you are working alone.

While a basic knowledge of SAS is assumed, SAS code and program examples will be given. It is assumed that the reader has some experience with the SAS DATA step and SAS procedure syntax.

Introduction

Data Analysis Plans 3

Data Analysis Plans

Before a builder begins to construct a home, a detailed blueprint or plan for the structure is drawn up to meet the aspirations and budget of the buyers. The blueprint is then modified and revised as necessary to fulfill the new home owners' needs, while also conforming to county, state, and federal building codes. The blueprint may also be revised after construction has begun, as the builder encounters unexpected situational barriers or the buyers request reasonable changes that they can afford to implement.

A data analysis plan is analogous to a blueprint, but instead of developing a house, you are developing a mutual understanding of questions, data, and methods for analysis. A data analysis plan is a detailed document outlining procedures for conducting an analysis on data, produced by the data analyst and presented and discussed with the project team.

Before beginning the data analysis plan, we encourage you to have a data policy document written if appropriate for your situation. This document, covered in Chapter 3, is comparable to building codes in that it defines common standards for conducting a project, from the point of engaging clients through data analysis and reporting.

There are different types of analysis plans for different purposes. One type, called a proposal analysis plan, is written in response to a solicitation for your services as part of a grant or contract proposal. The proposal analysis plan is written before data has been collected and usually includes critical information about how data will be collected. Generally speaking, proposal analysis plans are not detailed, but include sufficient information for a formal review team to understand the specific questions being asked and the method for analyzing data to answer these questions.

Proposal analysis plans are usually followed by a more detailed analysis plan if the work is awarded to the analysis group, and it is known that work will proceed. These detailed plans are often reviewed by outside experts such as a data monitoring committee (DMC) or a Data and Safety Monitoring Board (DSMB) in the case of clinical trials research and are the most extensive type of analysis plan. Therefore, all aspects of such plans are covered in this book.

However, analysis plans should also be written for more modest undertakings. Examples include studies of data already collected, such as data obtained through clinical trials whose primary results have already been published or data collected from observational studies. In fact, any time a research question is posed, an analysis plan should be written for it, no matter how small the question or how brief the plan.

Analysts often think that once the plan is written they are finished with planning, and may conduct the project through to the end without referring back to, or updating, the plan. To proceed in this manner, though, is to miss valuable opportunities to use the plan as a tool not only to guide analysis, but also as a tool for communicating with a client, ensuring that your results are of the highest quality and that results have been discussed and understood by your client.

An unappreciated value of an analysis plan is that it can serve to control expectations of what will be accomplished when the analysis is complete. Often clients have unreasonable expectations, and a plan can put reasonable limits on the scope of analyses. Without a plan, it is possible that analyses will continue until resources or patience are drained, and an endpoint is never reached.

Moreover, a plan can enable clear communication and understanding among team members. By detailing every aspect of the analysis in a written document, it enables all members to review it and then discuss the finer points. In this way, an analysis plan can open a dialogue that might never have taken place. When unanticipated events or aspects of a study are encountered, the plan should be updated, discussed with the client, and then analysis may resume. This cycle may continue to the extent allowed by analysis policy and by available resources, until the final results are obtained.

Some will argue that implementing an analysis plan in this way might limit exploration of the data and thus limit the capacity for discovery. It is true that there is a tradeoff between strictly following policies and plans on the one hand and the discoveries that are possible through unhindered data exploration. Seat-of-the-pants work can be reckless and wasteful. Yet an overly pedantic approach may bar the way to unexpected but useful discoveries. While we generally advise a vigilant approach and adherence to the plan, if the analyst does stray from the plan, the reasons and methods of doing so should be recorded in a revision of the plan.

Finally, the analysis plan can be used as a basis for a final report. As the plan is updated and refined, summary data and results may be inserted into the document. In this way, all steps are recorded. The end result will be a document of sufficient detail to support rapid reporting and sufficient transparency to guide subsequent studies aimed at replicating the findings and conclusions.

This book is meant to be an aid for all analysts but could also be used in a research methods course or a seminar on statistical consulting. Chapter 3 describes a policy document. It may not be relevant to small projects conducted in isolated settings, such as student term projects. An outline of a data analysis plan is given in Chapter 4. The remaining chapters explain how to write each section, how to begin to look at data, and how to continually update the data analysis plan, methodically populating each section with results until a final report is to be written.

3

Before the Plan: Develop an Analysis Policy

Summary 5
The Analysis Policy 6
   Overview 6
Analysis Policy Components 7
   Mission Statement 7
   Project Initiation 7
   Data Analysis Proposals 8
   Data Analysis Plans 8
   Data Policies 8
   Statistical Policies 9
   Reporting Guidelines 10
Analysis Policies for Large Projects 11
Example Project Analysis Policy 11
   Introduction 11
   TIAD Study Policies 12
References 14

Summary

This chapter is intended for analysts who work in a consistent setting where multiple analysis plans will be developed over an extended period of time, be they for external clients and large projects, or for clients who are internal to the analysts' own organization and having smaller projects. Analysis policies govern the rules of engagement between analyst and client, as well as principles of data handling and integrity, and statistical principles under which all analyses for all projects will be conducted.

The Analysis Policy

Overview

Before you hang a shingle to announce your services, you should invest the time to develop an analysis policy. If your shingle is already hung, there is no better time than the present to gather your colleagues to formulate policies. These policies will serve as your charter or rules for planning and conducting analyses. Analysis policies outline the standard practices that you, your organization, and all of your projects will follow for all analyses and all clients.

Analysis policies can serve to limit, and, more importantly, to focus client expectations early. Policies are especially important when working with clients who have little background in statistics. They may also prove valuable when working with experienced clients who are accustomed to getting their way, particularly when "their way" may be contrary to your professional principles. Reviewing policies with a client may also give you the opportunity to assess their level of understanding of standards and practices in your field of work. If there is a poor fit between client expectations and your policies, an early review of policies can save time and prevent ill feelings from developing.

A policy document may be cursory or very precise and extensive, depending on the size of your organization and scope of your practice area. The format and content should be customized to suit your needs and environment.

Though the degree of adherence to policy should be high for most projects, it may vary because there are some tradeoffs to consider. First, industry norms evolve. For example, the literature on a particular branch of inferential statistical methods may begin to favor previously unpopular approaches. If you find yourself using these methods more often, it may be time to revise your policies to allow or emphasize them. Second, policies that lie stale too long may stifle innovation. For example, strict limitations on data exploration can prevent unexpected yet important discoveries. The right balance must be found between adherence to policy and flexibility. However, for most projects we recommend erring on the side of adherence, particularly when managing the expectations of new clients.

An example of a simple policy document can be found at the end of this chapter. The components of your policy will vary according to your industry and the scope of your work and clientele. However, below are a few key sections that you should consider including.

Analysis Policy Components

Mission Statement

A policy document might start with a mission statement that formally and succinctly states your department's or your institution's aims and values. A statement or list of goals can also be included. This section allows prospective clients to promptly assess at a high level whether there is a mutual fit with your organization. For example, if your mission statement identifies you as a group that focuses on government sector clients who develop policies to advance the well-being of the general population, a private sector client wishing to create market penetration of a particular product without regard for general well-being will immediately be made aware of a potential mismatch.

Project Initiation

Following the mission statement, a policy document should indicate how an interested party should begin communications with your office in order to start a project. It guides clients to your front door and begins the interchange of client needs and policy information in an orderly fashion. Too often, casual conversations between potential clients and non-managerial staff can lead to premature meetings, unreasonable expectations, and implied commitments that must be unknotted before a proper relationship can begin. This is a common problem for law offices and professional consulting groups. Impatient clients wish to get answers or see a light at the end of the tunnel before policies have been conveyed, mutual fit assessed, and level of effort estimated.

Instruments such as information sheets and mandatory intake forms are very helpful in this regard. These are usually followed by a formal meeting where the previously provided written policies are verbally reviewed and explained if necessary. Conveying initiation policies up front, and requiring all staff to follow them will prevent work from launching too early. The vetting process will prevent back-tracking and save analysts from running in circles, wasting everyone's time and possibly eroding morale.

The project initiation section is also a good place to present your expectations of the roles to be played by all project collaborators. For example, if the analysts in your group intend to be the sole analysts for all projects, then you should say so here. Authorship expectations should also be covered. If you expect that data analysts will always be cited as co-authors for all peer-reviewed publications stemming from your work, this should be made clear in the project initiation section.

Data Analysis Proposals

Your policy document might state that a written proposal from the client to you will be required soon after your initial meeting. In it, the client states any questions they wish to address through the project, the data and general resources they might contribute, and their best description of the services they expect to receive from you.

The format and content of a typical proposal should fit your business scope and clientele. In your policy document, you should avoid making the need for a proposal appear off-putting to small or inexperienced clients. To this end, you might include an outline of a typical proposal in your policy document and make it clear that you are available to guide or participate in its development. Knowing in advance what you would like in a proposal will save both parties considerable time in the long run.

Depending on your business model, the proposal may lead to a binding contract. It is beyond the scope of this book to cover business contracts. However, data analysts rarely encounter these issues in their formal training and would do well to develop some knowledge and experience in the area of negotiations and business contracting.

Data Analysis Plans

Your policy document should state the requirement that an analysis plan will be mutually developed after or in conjunction with the analysis proposal. The analysis plan may also eventually be incorporated into a contract, again depending on your business practices. The development and execution of this plan is the main thrust of this book. An outline or template of a typical analysis plan may be included in your policy document, though it should be clear to potential clients that the plan is not required until after initial meetings.

The policy document should explain the rationale for having an analysis plan. The following should be clear from this section:

- Analyses will not begin until all parties agree to the analysis plan.,
- Deviation from the original plan may require amendments to the previous version of the analysis plan.
- Significant changes to the original plan may require additional negotiations.

Data Policies

In this section of your policy document you should make potential clients aware of requirements that govern data handled by your organization, including but not limited to the following:

- privacy and security requirements, as applicable, established by
    - governments
    - other relevant non-governmental organizations or project partners

- your own organization
- acceptable methods and formats for data exchange between you, the client, and other project partners
- data ownership and stewardship and formal documents that may be required in this regard
- data use and transfer agreements, as required

In the case of human subjects research and in other circumstances, approval for data collection and/or exchange must come from a recognized committee such as an Internal Review Board (IRB). Analysts working in the field of medical research are well acquainted with these requirements, but the public and many inexperienced clients are not well versed in the details. They may not even recognize that data for their proposed project requires IRB approval for inter-party data exchange and analysis. Your policy document is a good place to raise this issue.

Statistical Policies

The section covering statistical policies should not be a statistical primer, but it should lay out general rules for analysis and interpretation. Reviewing these polices with the client before analysis begins serves to control expectations. The policies cover situations that usually are not part of the analysis proposal, analysis plan, or contracts described above. You should cover topics that have been an issue in the past or are known to crop up frequently in your field of work. Some examples of statistical policies you might consider for inclusion in your policy document are listed below.

- State your policies that govern missing data and imputation. Two examples:
  - Missing data will not be ignored. At a minimum you will test for how missing data may bias your sample *(Ghosh, 2008) (Sterne, 2009)*.
  - Indicate that in longitudinal data analysis, you will shy away from biased procedures such as last observation carried forward (Chandan, 2009).
- Describe your position on the appropriateness and circumstances of subgroup analysis and your policy for conducting unplanned post hoc analysis. Clients not trained in statistics often have a great deal of difficulty understanding why it is a violation of statistical assumptions to limit analyses in these ways. If planned analyses fail to give the desired results, some clients will pressure analysts to perform unplanned analyses until desired results are achieved. It is wise to anticipate and address these circumstances in your policy document.
  - Define the difference between a pre-specified subgroup analysis and a hypothesis-generating, post-hoc analysis and caution against making broad, unconstrained conclusions (Wang, 2007).
  - Consider referencing one or more journal articles that support your policies. This is a very effective way of lending credence to your positions.

- Emphasize that problems with subgroup analysis include increased probability of type I error when the null is true, decreased power when the alternative hypothesis is true, and difficulty in interpretation.
- If you are testing hypotheses,
  - State how you normally set type I and II error rates.
  - State that tests are normally 2-sided and under what circumstances you would use a 1-sided test.
  - Disclose requirements for including definitions of practical importance (referred to as clinical significance in medical research).
  - Communicate how you typically handle multiple comparisons and adjustment for type 1 error.
    - Some analysts adjust type 1 errors only for tests of the primary outcome.
    - In some cases, adjustment for type 1 errors involves a Bonferroni correction or an alternative such as the Holm-Bonferroni method (Abdi, 2010).
- If you are analyzing randomized clinical trials data, it is advisable to state that you will always use intention to treat (ITT) analyses in order to avoid bias from cross-overs, drop-outs, and non-compliance.

Reporting Guidelines

Below are some common examples of reporting guidelines that may be covered in a policy document.

- Address statistical significance and the interpretation of *p*-values. Note that a *p*-value cannot determine if a hypothesis is true and cannot determine if a result is important. You may want to reference the American Statistical Association's statement on this topic (Wasserstein and Lazar, 2016).
- Indicate whether you require reporting of confidence intervals, probability values (*p-value*), or both. Some clients resist proper reporting when the results are close to what the client does or does not wish them to be.
- Present your conventions for reporting the number of decimal places for data and *p*-values. For example, is it your policy to report 2 or 3 decimal places? In some fields (e.g. genomics), it is customary to report 10 or even 12 decimal places.
- State that you will report maximum and minimum values to the same number of decimal places as the raw data values, if that is your policy.
- State that means and medians will be reported to one additional decimal place and that standard deviations and standard errors will be reported to two places more than collected, if that is your policy.

Analysis Policies for Large Projects

To this point, we have framed analysis planning as having two tiers–the policy document to provide high-level guidance for all clients and all analyses and the analysis plan to provide specific guidance for a single analysis or closely linked analyses. However, well-established analytical centers may serve one or more very large projects spanning years or decades and resulting in dozens or hundreds of individual analyses. Examples abound in the realm of federally funded medical research. A typical case is the Adolescent Medicine Trials Network (ATN) for HIV/AIDS Intervention funded by the National Institute of Child Health and Human Development (NICHD) (NIH Eunice Kennedy Shriver National Institute of Child Health and Human Development, 2015). Another is the Nurses Health Study (www.nurseshealthstudy.org, 2016) which began in 1976, expanded in 1989, and continues into 2016.

In such cases, the two tiers policy and plans, may not serve the large project very well. The project may be so large that it functions as a semi-independent entity that requires its own policies to achieve congruency with collaborating institutions. Furthermore, many of the analyses under the project umbrella may share detailed criteria that do not properly belong in an institutional policy, yet it would be awkward to repeat them in all dozens or hundreds of analysis plans. An example would be how body mass index (BMI) is to be categorized in all analyses for a large obesity research program.

The solution is to add a middle tier, the project analysis policy. It should incorporate all key elements of the home institution's overarching analysis policy, as well as detailed criteria shared by many of the anticipated analyses. These detailed criteria are in essence promoted to the level of policy within the project, and need not be repeated in all analysis plans. Instead, analysis plans should make reference to the project policy. However, it is essential to keep all partners, particularly those who join after the project inauguration, aware of these policies through the life of the project.

Example Project Analysis Policy

Introduction

This is an example of a project analysis policy written by a group of analysts at a university-based research data analysis center. They are the statistical consulting group for a federally funded, nationwide, multi-institutional fictional study called Targeting Inflammation Using Athelis for Type 2 Diabetes (TIAD). These policies were written to provide guidance to non-statistical collaborators from around the nation on how to interact with the data coordinating center and what to expect when proposing analyses that will lead to publications in peer-reviewed journals.

The example is briefer than a policy document would be for a larger organization dealing with many clients who are unfamiliar with the service group and/or statistical analyses in general. We have foregone a mission statement because all collaborating institutions are fully aware of TIAD's purpose.

TIAD Study Policies

Project Initiation

All TIAD analyses intended to result in manuscripts will be tracked on the TIAD website. As each manuscript task progresses, its website entry will be populated with an analysis plan; manuscript drafts including all data tables and figures; and all correspondence to and from journals. All documents must have dates and version numbers.

Statisticians from the data coordinating center will always be cited as co-authors on each manuscript. Disagreements about statistical methods or interpretations of statistical results will be openly discussed among co-authors and the publications committee members. However, consistent with the roles identified in the original federal grant application, the statisticians of the study coordinating center will make final determinations on analysis methods and interpretations.

Data Analysis Proposals

Proposals for manuscripts must be submitted to our group via the TIAD website and addressed to our group for review by the TIAD publications committee, whose membership is identified on the website. Data coordinating center staff are available to assist with proposal development.

Each proposal must include the following:

- Study Title
- Primary Author and contact information
- Collaborators and co-authors who will participate in the work, and what their roles will be
- Objective (A brief description of the analysis—may include primary and secondary questions or hypotheses)
- Rationale (Describe how results from this analysis will impact the topic area)
- Study design (Summarize the study design, such as matched case-control, nested case-control, descriptive, etc.)
- Sample description (Define inclusion and exclusion criteria and outcomes)
- Resources (Describe resources that may be required such as laboratory measurements that may be beyond what is normally expected)

- Give a brief data analysis plan (Include power and sample size estimates)

Data Analysis Plan

Each manuscript task must have a data analysis plan before any analyses are conducted. A data analysis plan is a detailed document outlining procedures for conducting an analysis on data. They will be drafted by the data analyst based on the research questions identified in the proposal. Plans will be discussed in order to foster mutual understanding of questions, data, and methods for analysis. Analysis plans are intended to ensure quality, but also to put reasonable limits on the scope of analyses to be conducted and to preserve resources in the pursuit of the agreed upon endpoint. Finally, each analysis plan will serve as the outline and starting point for manuscript development.

- Plans will be written in conjunction with the data coordinating center, but only after the proposal has been approved by the publications committee.
- Working with the study group chair, the coordinating center statistician will draft the plan. It will define the data items to be included in the analysis and describe the statistical methods used to answer the primary and secondary questions.
- The study group will review and approve the plan or suggest revisions.
- Deviations from the original approved analysis plan will be added to the document to create a new version of the analysis plan.
- Significant changes to the original plan may require approval by the publications committee.

Data Policies

- Local IRB approval is required from the institutions of all investigators.
- Data will remain in secure control of the data coordinating center and will not be distributed to investigators.

Statistical Policies

- Analyses will adhere to the original study design and use methods appropriate for randomized clinical trials.
- All analyses comparing the TIAD treatment groups will be conducted under the principle of intention-to-treat (ITT), with all patients included in their originally assigned TIAD treatment group.
- Methods that require deletion of subjects or visits will be avoided, as they break the randomization and introduce biases.
- Analyses will be either 1) conducted separately by treatment group, or 2) adjusted for treatment effects. Analyses including more than one treatment group will initially include tests for treatment group interactions with other factors because of the TIAD's reported effects of the active treatment on most outcomes.

- Subgroups will be defined from baseline characteristics rather than outcomes. Subgroup analyses will be interpreted cautiously and will follow the guidelines presented in Wang et al., 2007.
- Retrospective case-control studies will be deemed appropriate when the study lacks power for prospective analysis, for example when an outcome is extremely rare or when its ascertainment is very expensive and cannot be obtained for the entire study cohort.
- All results that are nominally significant at the 0.05 level will be indicated.
- Hochberg's improved Bonferroni procedure will be used to adjust for multiple comparisons where appropriate (1988).

Reporting

- We will not report cell sample sizes less than 10 in tables.
- We will use the following categorization for race: African American, American Indian, Asian American/Pacific Islander, Caucasian.
- Latino ethnicity will be reported separately from race categories.
- Age categories will be defined as follows: <18, 18 to <25, 25 to <30, 30 to <35, and 35 and older.
- We will use the World Health Organization definition for BMI (kg/m^2) classification:
  - <18.5 Underweight
  - 18.50-24.99 Normal range
  - 25.00 to <30.00 Overweight
  - ≥30.00 Obese

References

Abdi, Herve. *Holm's Sequential Bonferroni Procedure*. Thousand Oaks, CA: Sage2010.

Chandan, Saha, and Michael P. Jones. "Bias in the Last Observation Carried Forward Method Under Informative Dropout." *Journal of Statistical Planning and Inference* 139 (2)2009: 246–55.

Ghosh, Sunita, and Punam Pahwa. "Assessing Bias Associated With Missing Data from Joint Canada/U.S. Survey of Health: An Application." Proceedings of the Survey Research Methods Section, ASA 2008; JSM 2008; 3394-3401. **http://www.amstat.org/meetings/jsm/2008/onlineprogram/index.cfm?fuseaction=abstract_details=302187**

Hochberg, Yosef. "A Sharper Bonferroni Procedure for Multiple Tests of Significance." *Biometrika* 75 (4)1988: 800–802.

Peduzzi, P., Wittes, J., Detre, K. and Holford, T. "Analysis as-Randomized and the Problem of Non-adherence: An Example from the Veterans Affairs Randomized Trial of Coronary Artery Bypass Surgery." Statist. Med. (12) 1993: 1185–1195.

Sterne, Jonathan A.C. Ian R. White, John B. Carlin, Michael Spratt, Patrick Royston, Michael G. Kenward, Angela M. Wood, and James R. Carpenter. *Multiple Imputation for Missing Data in Epidemiological and Clinical Research: Potential and Pitfalls.* BMJ 2009; 33. **http://www.bmj.com/content/338/bmj.b2393**

Wang, Rui, Stephen W. Lagakos, James H. Ware, David J. Hunter, and Jeffrey M. Drazen. "Statistics in Medicine – Reporting of Subgroup Analyses in Clinical Trials." *New England Journal of Medicine* 357 (21)2007: 2189-2194.

Wasserstein, Ronald L. Nicole A. Lazar. "The ASA's Statement on p-Values; Context, Process, and Purpose." *The American Statistician* 40 (2)2016: 129-133.

4

Outline of a Plan

Summary 17
Outline of a Typical Plan 18
    Introduction 18
    Hypotheses or Questions 18
    Data Description 18
    Exploring the Data 18
    General Statistical Approach 18
    Analysis of Questions/Hypotheses 19
    State Potential Conclusions and List Weaknesses 19
    Timeline 19

Summary

The plan is a working document that changes often over the life the investigation, but within the parameters of the agreed upon policy. This chapter presents an outline of what might be contained in a plan, but the analyst should reorganize it as necessary, and include or exclude sections to fit the needs of the investigation. An example of a data analysis plan is provided in Chapter 12.

Outline of a Typical Plan

Introduction

In this section, plainly state the purpose of the study, the objectives, hypotheses or questions, and the aims of the analysis. A brief background describing previous work on the topic may also be given to set the stage. The investigative team should be named and their roles identified. Finally, identify and describe the target audience for the final report.

Hypotheses or Questions

Clearly state the hypotheses or questions. The next chapter explains how these are distinguished from each other, and how they relate to the objectives and aims. If secondary questions such as subgroup analyses are planned, they should be covered in this section as well.

Data Description

In this part of the plan, describe the source of the data. This is a straightforward task for secondary data analyses and for primary data analyses where the data has already been collected and is available. For situations where the data has not yet been collected, describe the data as it is foreseen. But make it clear that adjustments may be required if the data does not materialize on the schedule or in the form that is expected. In your description, include potential sources of bias, inclusion and exclusion criteria, case and control definitions if applicable, outcome definitions, and definitions for all relevant variables.

Exploring the Data

Assuming you have some data in-hand, use this section to begin exploring the data. Begin to look at distributions. Include plots to identify outliers and determine sources of variations. You may want to include a preliminary description of the data such as a baseline (study starting point) table in this section.

General Statistical Approach

In this portion of the plan, identify rules and assumptions of the analyses to follow. If you have a data policy statement covering these matters, then include it in an appendix. As applicable to your analysis, define type 1 and type 2 error thresholds, sample size requirements and statistical power, planned adjustments for covariates, how missing data and correlated independent variables will be handled, plans for sensitivity analysis, and finally how you plan to present the results. If multiple hypothesis testing and multiple comparisons are planned, then state the method you will use to adjust type 1 errors in these situations.

Analysis of Questions/Hypotheses

For each hypothesis or question that was previously identified, state the statistical method you will use (e.g., linear regression, Poisson regression, etc.) to answer the question. Explicitly state all assumptions required for the analysis to be appropriate for the task and list covariates if any. Be sure to explain statistical concepts in a way that a non-statistician can understand them.

State Potential Conclusions and List Weaknesses

Discuss the potential conclusions you think may be made when the analysis is complete. Explain how each may advance or reframe the literature on the subject matter, and, in the case of clinical or public health studies, how the results might inform healthcare delivery or policy. This discussion should include potential weaknesses of the study.

Timeline

Present a timeline for completing the analysis. Allocate time for discussion and revisions.

The Plan Introduction

Summary 21
Objectives, Hypotheses or Questions, and Aims 22
    Introduction 22
    Objectives 22
    Hypotheses 22
    Questions 23
    Aims 23
Identify the Project Team 24
Identify the Target Audience 25

Summary

Set the stage for the analysis plan by stating the objective or purpose, hypotheses or questions to be addressed, and the specific aims of the investigation. In addition, the introduction identifies who will work on the study and in what capacity, and where the study results will ultimately be presented if public presentation is appropriate and expected. As an analyst, you may have already discussed these matters with the project team. But putting them in writing and in your own words is an opportunity to clarify any misunderstandings. Often members of the team have different ideas about the scope of the study, so it is important to agree on the aims and objectives up front. Moreover, this gives the analyst an opportunity to step foot into the realm of the investigative team's field. Much of this information may have been presented somewhat vaguely in a proposal, but re-stating it here in concise but specific language will help to focus the team and the upcoming work.

Objectives, Hypotheses or Questions, and Aims

Introduction

Objectives are the broader reasons or purposes for the undertaking. Hypotheses are proposed explanations for observable phenomena. Research questions pertain to exploratory studies where the outcome is not necessarily predictable. Aims are the general methods or approaches that will be used to test the hypotheses or explore the research questions.

Objectives

Open with a brief statement about the purpose of the inquiry. The objective or purpose of the study is its potential significance and impact on the field in the case of scientific investigation, or on the client's strategy or operations if you are working for a commercial or advocacy group. Here are some examples of objectives:

- Test a new drug intervention to reduce blood-sugar levels in patients with diabetes.
- Determine which is the best among common methods for eradicating the mosquito vector for dengue fever.
- Determine the most effective outreach method for encouraging residents of impoverished villages in sub-Saharan African countries to register for a new United Nations assistance program.
- Determine which states are best candidates for federal-state partnerships to pilot a new military veterans benefits program intended to replace several existing programs.

Follow the objective with a statement of the significance of the problem noting the relevance of this work for the field in which the study is being conducted. A summary of the current knowledge with references provides a foundation for the rationale for conducting the investigation. Identify any gaps in knowledge that this study might address, and convey how the work will help to fill such gaps.

Hypotheses

Studies are set up to address either hypotheses, which are based on existing theories, or research questions, which are purely exploratory in nature. It is more common for research projects to be based on hypotheses because they are more closely tied to established science, which means they are driven by previously established knowledge or best practices. They are more likely to contribute to a body of knowledge, and a statistical probability can be estimated for their findings.

Most people tend to think of hypotheses as being associated only with "scientific" studies. However, explicitly stated hypotheses are necessary and appropriate for any study where there is an expected outcome that can be refuted by evidence, even if the domain of investigation is not a classic field of science. For example, your client may be an advocacy group focused on resettlement of immigrant refugees. Studies of other populations have suggested to them that a new method of outreach through social media is more effective than traditional media in encouraging refugees to register for available services. With proper data collection and analysis, this may be a refutable claim and thus qualifies as a hypothesis. Some example hypotheses are as follows:

- Drug A can safely and effectively reduce blood sugar in diabetic patients.
- Pamphlets distributed at food markets are more effective than broadcast or print media advertisements in increasing the rate of pre-registration for a new vaccine in impoverished villages.

Questions

Not all endeavors have an expected outcome that is refutable. Some are simply exploratory in nature, and research questions are more suitable than hypotheses. Some examples are as follows:

- In lower income neighborhoods, which intervention is most effective at reducing the mosquito vector for dengue fever: 1) an educational program aimed at preventing standing pools of water, 2) subsidies for mosquito nets and window screen maintenance, or 3) traditional chemical fogging programs?
- Which states have combined military veteran populations that are most representative of the national veteran population, and whose combined veteran populations suggest that pilot participation of those states would approach but not exceed the federal dollars allotted for a five-year pilot program?

Aims

An aim describes how the study team will address the hypothesis or question. There may be more than one aim per question. However, each aim should be directly linked to a specific hypothesis or question. The following aims might be appropriate for the example hypotheses and questions, above:

- We will conduct a randomized clinical trial of drug A versus currently accepted treatments with drugs B and C to determine if A is equally safe yet more effective in reducing blood-sugar levels in pre-diabetic patients.
- We will conduct a randomized trial of 25 remote villages, clustered by tribal affiliation, to determine which of three outreach methods result in the highest rate of pre-registration for a new vaccine: 1) pamphlets distributed by community merchants at food markets, 2) local radio advertisements, or 3) print media advertisements.

- We will conduct a prospective cohort study of lower income neighborhoods to determine which of three interventions is most effective at reducing the mosquito vector for dengue fever: 1) an educational program aimed at preventing standing pools of water, 2) subsidies for mosquito nets and window screen maintenance, or 3) traditional chemical fogging programs?

- We will conduct an iterative series of observational analyses and actuarial projections to identify the set of U.S. states most suitable for a five-year federal-state partnership pilot for a veterans benefit program. Observational statistics from existing veterans databases will serve as baseline data for the actuarial projections of total veterans who meet the demographic and socioeconomic eligibility criteria and are who are most likely to enroll in the new program. Iterative analyses will proceed until the set of states is identified that best represents the national veteran population and whose projected pilot program costs will not exceed allocated funds.

Identify the Project Team

In a table, list the full name, degrees, and affiliations of each member. Also list the role that each one is expected to fulfill. In most circumstances, it is best to identify the project lead, who is usually the main author if publications are to ensue. Stating the names and roles of each member at the outset avoids problems down the road.

It is surprising how common are misunderstandings about roles. An illustration in academia is assumptions that are made about authorship of publications resulting from the work. For example, junior statisticians who assist in analysis may hope for or expect to be credited as authors while other team members may think differently. Less experienced clinicians may not envision authorship for any of the statisticians. Senior team members may not plan to credit the data collection and processing staff. Journals sometimes provide guidance for defining authorship-worthy contributions. If so, the guidance should be consulted at this time.

Beyond credits, the project team table should define responsibilities for each team member. The responsibilities included in the table should be as comprehensive as possible. For example, if a data collection and processing staff is identified as well as the statisticians/ analysts, the two groups may assume that the other will take responsibility for data cleaning unless arrangements are made in advance and indicated in the table.

The project team table can be expanded to include other information as appropriate. This might be contact information, estimates of level of effort (e.g., full-time equivalencies), and the identity of back-up or support staff for some or all roles.

The table below presents some common roles and responsibilities to consider including. Small projects may have only two or three persons listed and only a handful of roles and responsibilities dispersed among them. Large projects may list many persons and include roles, responsibilities, and other details not listed here. The responsibilities listed here are only notional and may be redistributed among roles or changed as appropriate for your situation.

Table 5.1 Common Project Team Roles and Responsibilities

Role	Responsibility
Principal investigator/project director	Principal subject matter expert; responsible for the overall project and final product(s); primary author of publications; responsible for adherence to human subjects research requirements
Co-investigator	Additional subject matter expert; assists principal in all responsibilities
Lead statistician/analyst	Develops study design; drafts analysis plan; leads or conducts all quantitative analyses; interprets findings for investigators; writes methods and findings sections of reports and publications
Junior statistician	Assists lead statistician in all matters; performs final data cleaning efforts
Data collection roles	Collects raw data (e.g., laboratory, survey, or clinical data) or acquires secondary data (e.g., public or commercial files for secondary data analysis)
Data preparation and processing roles	Converts data to a form usable by programmers and/or statisticians; responsible for initial data cleaning
Programmer	May write and execute computer programs for any project stage or task, including data capture, processing, cleaning, analysis, or reporting.
Editor/illustrator	Edits manuscripts and reports; assists principal investigator with publication

Identify the Target Audience

An ultimate goal of any investigation is to disseminate the results to some audience. However, just as unstated assumptions about roles can lead to trouble downstream, so too can misunderstandings about the targeted audience. The target audience may be a small group internal to your organization, the management staff of the client's commercial enterprise, academics or clinicians in a particular branch of study, public policy decision makers, or even the general public.

While disagreements regarding audience scope are rare, the details of dissemination are often subject to differences. For example, the client or principal investigator may want to exercise complete control over whether and how results are disseminated. He or she may wish to bury negative findings or findings that are contrary to his or her beliefs. Alternatively, if the findings are auspicious he or she may want to attempt publication in a highly prestigious journal that is not likely to take interest in a modest study. Analysts and statisticians, on the other hand, may wish to publish any findings in any journal in order to grow their curriculum vitae and support academic job security.

These can be difficult matters to discuss, and hence are too often put aside. We strongly recommend that they be openly addressed in the introductory section of the analysis plan, even to the extent of identifying appropriate journals or other venues, reviewing the requirements of those venues, and summarizing why the results might be of interest to the targeted audience.

6

Hypotheses, Questions, and Study Design

Summary	27
Conceptualizing the Problem	28
Hypotheses	29
Research Questions	29
Study	29
Type of Study	29
Cases and Controls	30
Inclusion and Exclusion	30
Specify Outcomes	31
Identifying Confounders	31
Communicating with the Study Team	32

Summary

The foundation of an analysis plan is a clear statement of the hypotheses or research questions to be addressed. This chapter outlines how hypotheses are formulated. In this section of your plan you should also cover the study design, inclusion and exclusion criteria, case and control definitions if conducting a trial, outcome definitions, and key variable definitions.

Conceptualizing the Problem

All scientific inquiry begins with a problem in mind. Framing the problem the right way is imperative for clear thinking, proper planning and effective communication. Problems should be specific and contain four essential parts:

1 A population. Conclusions will be applicable to this population.

2 Effects — the cause or causes of interest.

3 A comparison group or factor.

4 An outcome of interest.

As an example a client may have experienced a sharp increase in medical insurance premiums because the insurance company has detected unusually high levels of back-related diagnoses and procedures among company employees. The client wishes to reduce the rate of back problems and may frame the problem as a need to understand all the risk factors for back pain. This is too general; it only specifies an outcome, back pain. It could lead to a fishing expedition and a waste of time and resources.

Based on knowledge of this specific workplace, a better request might be, "Can we determine if activities in our workplace are associated with an elevated risk of lower back pain occurring among our employees?" This problem statement contains the four essential elements defined above.

1 The population is employees

2 The effect is activities in the workplace

3 The comparison is factors outside the workplace

4 The outcome is presence/absence of back pain

Problems are presented in the analysis plan as either hypotheses or research questions. It is not always possible to develop hypotheses, but they should be used whenever possible because the statistical methods and results of hypothesis-driven analyses are more robust and informative.

Hypotheses

Hypotheses are used when the science surrounding the problem is more established and there is reason to believe that a proposed relationship between variables approximates the truth. A hypothesis is a statement describing something that can be tested. Testing may be done through observation or an experiment. The hypothesis will state the answer to the question that is being tested. Evidence must be given to support the hypothesis. To form a hypothesis, choose an outcome or dependent variable that will be measured. Then choose factors or independent variables that will predict response in the outcome variable.

The question above "Can we determine if activities in our workplace are associated with an elevated risk of lower back pain occurring among our employees?" might be replaced with a hypothesis if the employer has noticed that employees whose job descriptions require lifting of packages tend to miss work more often due to backaches. The simple statement of hypothesis might be "The incidence of lower back pain is more common among our employees who are required to lift packages as part of their duties."

Research Questions

We use research questions when there is little prior knowledge to draw on and thus possible cause-and-effect relationships between variables do not suggest themselves or are very tenuous. Continuing with the previous example, our employer client might not be aware of any differences between employees who do and do not report back problems. Furthermore, none of the company job descriptions call for activities that would seem to be risk factors for back pain, and the literature on occupational hazards in this industry is mute on the issue of back pain. Therefore exploratory research is called for. The research question might be, "Among our employees are any of the following demographic, social, work activity or work environment factors, solely or in combination, associated with higher incidence of back pain?".

Study

Type of Study

Define whether the study will be **experimental** or **observational**. Whenever possible **experimental** studies are preferred because we may be more confident in their conclusions.

In experimental studies an intervention, program, or treatment is purposefully applied to the experimental units or subjects and the effects are observed. For example an investigator may wish to study the effectiveness of a new method for teaching reading. Reading teachers may be randomly assigned to use the new method or the traditional approach, and after a period of time their students are tested for reading comprehension and improvement from baseline scores.

State whether the study is a randomized controlled trial (RCT), where assignment of the experimental units to treatment groups is controlled by the research team, or if it is a quasi-experimental study, where differential exposure occurs among the units but is not controlled by the research team. Clinical trials of drugs are a common example of RCTs. Examples of quasi-experimental studies are researching the effects of a government policy change or a natural disaster.

If RCT randomization to an intervention is planned, describe the randomization process in detail. These descriptions are not only useful for understanding the study but will also be useful when writing the final report.

An **observational** study is one in which the subjects are observed and no intervention or treatment is given although measurements may be taken. Observational studies generally fall into three categories: 1) cross-sectional studies, such as surveys of public attitude, 2) cohort studies that prospectively follow a group of subjects to measure exposures and developmental outcomes, and 3) case-control studies such as those that retrospectively compare subjects with a condition to those who lack it for differences in exposures or experiences in order to understand the relationship between exposure and condition.

Cases and Controls

Defining and identifying cases and controls in case-control studies is a special challenge for many inexperienced analysts. The definitions should be clear and specific so that anyone replicating the study could satisfactorily identify similar cases and controls. Typically a case is identified as having a disease or condition and a control is free of the condition. Matched case-control studies are particularly powerful because the statistical methods can better control for the factors upon which case-control subject pairs are matched. If matching is done state what variables were used in the matching, and whether matching was done directly on raw variable value, levels of variable values, or if frequency matching was done. Also report the ratio of cases to controls. This information will be needed to select appropriate analysis methods.

Inclusion and Exclusion

Describe the population and the sample included in the study. For example, a study may be conducted in patients with diabetes (the population) and subjects will be recruited from specified clinics (sample). Define the criteria by which observations were included and were excluded. If there is a long list of criteria, consider listing them in a table for a clear presentation.

Specify Outcomes

Primary

Clearly and concisely define the primary outcome of the study. A primary outcome in an observational cohort study is the disease or condition following an exposure. In an experimental study, this is the crucial measurement used to assess the effect of an experimental variable. In a clinical study, it is the outcome measure demonstrates the therapeutic effect. In the example analysis plan, the primary outcome is clearly defined as change in HbA1c at week 48 in the intent-to-treat population.

Secondary

List and define any secondary outcomes that the study should investigate. These are events of interest that the study is not specifically designed or powered to investigate. If the primary outcome is a composite endpoint, meaning several events make up the endpoint, the individual components are often tested as secondary endpoints.

Results of secondary outcomes are to be interpreted with caution; the investigation was not designed to answer these questions. It is more likely that results are due to chance. By clearly listing and defining in the analysis plan and discussing these with the study team, there will not be any ambiguity about reporting outcomes as primary or secondary in the final, reporting stage. This will avoid the situation in which a secondary outcome reaches statistical significance while the primary does not, and the team would like to emphasize this result in the final report as if it were the primary outcome. Secondary endpoint results are used to help interpret results from testing the primary endpoint or to provide information for future research and should never be given the same consideration as the primary endpoint.

Subgroup analyses should be pre-specified in this section. Pre-specifying the analysis of subgroups helps to avoid pressure to analyze the data in many ways to find a positive result. Analysis and re-analysis increases the risk that a result may occur by chance alone. .

Identifying Confounders

This may be a good time to brainstorm with the project team about confounding. These are variables that correlate directly with both the outcome variable and the predictor variables. The study team is the best group to help you sort this out. For example, in a study, the question may be "is maternal smoking a risk factor of perinatal death?" The association is confounded by drinking alcohol. Smoking is associated with drinking alcohol which is associated with perinatal mortality. Drinking alcohol is associated with smoking, but could smoking have a direct toxic effect causing perinatal mortality? Alcohol consumption is a confounder variable. It is important for the analyst to be aware of confounder variables before analyzing data.

Communicating with the Study Team

The research questions and hypotheses are formulated with input from the investigational team. However, we have found that more often than not, you will initially work more closely with one or two members of the team. Therefore, it is essential that you circulate the questions and hypotheses for feedback from the entire team. You do not want to proceed until every member has signed off on them. Otherwise, you open up the possibility that you must repeat analyses as the question is reframed by a member of the team who was left out of the original discussion. Considerable time may be wasted as you reanalyze the data.

7

Data Description

Summary 33
Data Sources 33
    Data Not in Hand 33
    Data in Hand 34
    Reading the Data 34
Data Definitions 35
Data Summary 36
Reviewing the Data with the Study Team 37

Summary

Identify the source of the data, and validate it to the extent possible. Define all key variables and check their ranges and distributions for reasonableness. Meet with the study team to review the data and confirm that the variables relate to the study questions as expected.

Data Sources

Data Not in Hand

For situations where the data has not yet been collected or delivered to you, describe the data as it is foreseen, making clear that adjustments may be required if the data does not materialize on the schedule or in the form expected. Describe any bureaucratic or regulatory clearances that may be required, such as formal data use agreements or human-subjects research training and certification. Neither you nor your client should lose sight of such requirements because they can cause inopportune delays if forgotten.

Identify the organization or project that will deliver the data, along with the expected population or sample size and as much descriptive information about key variables as possible. If relevant descriptive statistics from the data have been published, such as means, frequency distributions, and ranges, include those statistics in this section of the plan. Cite any previous publications that used the data. It may prove handy to have those citations here when writing the final report.

Data in Hand

For situations where you have the data files in hand, it is also good practice to cite previous publications, and attempt to validate the published descriptive statistics. If you cannot replicate published statistics, it probably means you do not have the data you expected, or errors were made in the published analyses. Investigate and resolve discrepancies with those who conducted the previous analyses and delivered the data to you.

If the files are members of a family of files (e.g., multiple research protocols conducted under one study name, or a recurring data gathering project like the Census Bureau's American Communities Survey), provide the details of your files such as protocol number, date, and/or date range. In long-term clinical research projects, it is common to "lock" the data at various time points for interim or final analyses. The lock date should be noted. Document when, how, and from whom you received data. An example might be "The data file was copied to our department's secure FTP server on 12/31/2015 by Stacey Benson of Utah Toxicology Labs." All of these details are important to support your final write-up but also for ensuring that your analyses can be replicated by others if necessary.

Reading the Data

When you receive the data, it is a good practice to make a copy of it, placing the date of file "lock" or similarly unique identifying information in the new file name. If the data was not received in native SAS format, then document precisely how you converted it to SAS format by presenting your SAS code. Here is an example:

```
proc import data='test_measures_20151231.csv'
    out=labtests
    dbms=csv
    replace;
    getnames=yes;
    guessingrows=100;
RUN;
```

When text files are being read, errors often result from inadvertently truncated values. The statement 'guessingrows=100' reduces the likelihood of this happening by instructing SAS to use the first 100 datalines of the file to scan for the maximum width of variables. The default is 20. Make sure that you understand the implications of using different options for importing data in SAS.

This code, along with your description of the source data, should be verified by the group supplying the data. Including the SAS statements enables anyone verifying work to ensure that variables were read correctly.

Data Definitions

Include a table that lists all of the variables expected to be used in the analysis. A variable table may look like the one below.

Description	Definition	Data Type	Unit	Coding
Treatment group	assigned at randomization	Cat		0=active,1=placebo
Age	age at first screening	N	years	
Weight	weight at randomization	N	kg	
Height	standing height at randomization	N	cm	
BMI	body mass index, derived	N	kg/m^2	weight/height^2

Indicate which variables are derived from others, and how they were or will be derived. See BMI in the table for example.

This table can be simple or very detailed, depending on your needs. Provide the level of detail necessary to make sure that the study team understands which variables are included in the analysis. For example, there might be multiple body measurements taken at various times, but only the one taken at a particular stage is most appropriate for the question or hypothesis. Clarifying which measurement you intend to use will help the subject matter experts on your team ensure that the best value is used and spurious results are avoided.

You can use PROC CONTENTS to create the variable table. The contents can be entered into a table that you can then copy and paste into your analysis plan. For example, the following code will output a table of your data:

```
proc contents data = mydata out=datatab(keep=name type) noprint;
ods rtf file='datadef.rtf';
proc print data = datatab;
run;
```

```
ods rtf close;
ods listing;
```

In the example above and in many code examples to follow, we use SAS Output Delivery System (ODS) statements to open, write to, and then close rich text format (RTF) files. This file type is perfectly compatible with Microsoft Office applications such as Word. As you gain experience with SAS, you may develop a different workflow style. The out= option creates a data set with variable names and data types. It is then printed and can be pasted into your analysis plan document.

Data Summary

Once the data has been read into a SAS data set, you should summarize the data using appropriate summary statistics. This quick look at your data is not to ensure adequacy of the data for the inferential statistical analyses you may have in mind later on. Rather, it is to catch the most obvious data errors, which hopefully can be addressed with your file sources. Highlight outliers and ask the lab or data source to verify the data. At times, particularly if you are the first to analyze the data, corrections must be made by your source before you can proceed.

SAS has many options for producing summary statistics including the procedures FREQ, MEANS, SUMMARY, REPORT, SQL and UNIVARIATE to name a few. We prefer PROC UNIVARIATE for most initial data file examinations. The example below highlights values from a data set of lab values that may be of concern and require checking with the source:

```
proc univariate data = labtests outtable=out_labtests noprint;
  var _numeric_;
  run;
ods rtf file='datasum.rtf';
proc print data = out_labtests label noobs;
  var _var_ _min_ _p1_ _p10_ _q1_ _median_ _q3_ _p90_ _p95_ _p99_ _max_;
  run;
ods rtf close;
ods listing;
```

The outtable= option creates a data set with numerous statistics for variables specified in the var statement. In this case, we have requested statistics for all numeric variables using the _numeric_ keyword. For each variable, we have chosen to print the variable name (_var_), minimum, maximum, and various percentile and quantile values (_p'x'_ and _q'x'_), with the median value in the middle of the list.

Reviewing the Data with the Study Team

By now, you have defined the study, ensured that you have the correct data, and described the data. It is a good time to review your work with the entire study team. You may send the document out for review in advance, but do not accept email feedback in lieu of an in-person review. In our experience, there is no substitute for a live review.

Reviewing each variable definition with the team can be tedious. However, this is where the elements from the objectives and aims are operationalized. Final thoughts about research questions or hypotheses are hammered out. Team members may have made different assumptions, and it is important to reach consensus so that the final statistical tests are appropriate and meaningful. Discussion about the data at this time may lead to a revision in the research questions and hypotheses. It is far better to make these revisions now, early in the investigation, than to complete the analysis only to discover a variable was defined incorrectly or not in the best way.

8

Data Exploration

Summary 39
Descriptive Statistics for Major Variables 40
Exploring Outliers and Problematic Data Distributions 42
Distribution Problems 46
Determining the Source of Variability 49
Producing Baseline Tables 55
Communicating with the Project Team 57

Summary

This chapter covers preliminary descriptive analysis of the source data. The findings might reveal problems such as excessive missing data or truncated values that might require resourcing the data, rethinking the analyses, or even modifying the aims to fit analyses that can be done with the available data while remaining true to the hypotheses or study questions.

It may be difficult to decide how in-depth you want to go in describing the data. At this stage, the line between planning and analyzing starts to fade. Think back to the analogy of the blueprint used in constructing a house. Once the blueprint is made, it is revised to conform to building codes, landscape or geographical barriers, etc. The same is true with the analysis plan. As more is learned about data, the plan may have to be revised, and sometimes this may be a major revision.

Descriptive Statistics for Major Variables

This chapter illustrates data exploration using an example of a clinical study that will rely on both categorical and numeric variables. However, the path is comparable for other fields of investigation. The first step is to learn how much missing data there is. Some should be expected, but if there is a suspiciously high amount of missing data, you should refer back to your source to see if mistakes in data collection or processing were made and if some can be retrieved. In our example, we would ask participating clinics to go back to the medical charts to gather missing data.

For numeric variables, check to see if the mean values and distributions are different from what you expect. Here you can uncover misunderstandings about the units used for recording data, or errors in calculation of derived variables.

SAS provides several procedures for summarizing data, including PROC SUMMARY, PROC MEANS, PROC TABULATE, and PROC REPORT. The SUMMARY and MEANS procedures mimic each other, with the former defaulting output to a data set for further processing and the latter defaulting its output to the display.

Below we use PROC MEANS to display summary statistics on our four key numeric variables: age, weight, height and body-mass index (BMI). We have selected five summary statistics to be displayed at two decimal places, which is consistent with our analysis policies. We have requested number of cases (n), number of missing values (nmiss), minimum (min) and maximum (max) values, and median is (p50). Refer to the PROC MEANS documentation for a wide range of statistics from which to choose. Some may be more appropriate for your field of study and the inferential statistical tests you may have in mind for later analysis.

```
ODS listing close;
ODS rtf file= 'c:/temp/TIADsum.rtf';
proc means data = TIAD n nmiss min max p50 maxdec=2;
 var age weight height bmi;
 run;
ODS rtf close;
ODS listing;
```

The output table can easily be pasted into the analysis document. The table is below.

Figure 8.1 Output from PROC MEANS for Checking Numerical Data

Variable	Label	N	N Miss	Minimum	Maximum	50th Pctl
Age	Age at randomization, y	280	0	23.52	74.04	44.61
Weight	Weight, kg	280	0	35.74	163.60	108.18
Height	Height, m	280	0	148.68	209.33	179.91
BMI	BMI, kg/m^2	280	0	.11	.63	.33

After you review the table with the project team, it becomes clear that something is wrong with the variable BMI. Its values are far too low. An inspection of the SAS code used to calculate it (not shown) reveals that there was an error in the formula for this derived variable. Height had been measured in centimeters, not meters. We make the correction by multiplying raw values by 100 and then produce a corrected table.

Figure 8.2 PROC MEANS Output Showing Corrected Numerical Data

Variable	Label	N	N Miss	Minimum	Maximum	50th Pctl
Age	Age at randomization, y	280	0	23.52	74.04	44.61
Weight	Weight, kg	280	0	35.74	163.60	108.18
Height	Height, m	280	0	148.68	209.33	179.91
BMI	BMI, kg/m^2	280	0	11.03	63.35	32.96

For categorical variables, PROC FREQ with a format statement produces tables that are easily pasted into the analysis document, ready for review.

```
proc format;
   value sex_  1='Male'
               2='Female';
   Value tx_   0='Active'
               1='Placebo';
run;
ODS listing close;

ODS rtf file = "c:/temp/TIADcatsum.rtf";
proc freq data = TIAD;
   tables sex tx;
   format sex sex_. tx tx_. ;
   run;
ODS rtf close;
```

42 Chapter 8 / Data Exploration

```
ODS listing;
```

Figure 8.3 Output from PROC FREQ to Check Categorical Data

		Sex			
sex	Frequency	Percent	Cumulative Frequency	Cumulative Percent
Male	153	54.64	153	54.64
Female	127	45.36	280	100.00

		Treatment Group			
tx	Frequency	Percent	Cumulative Frequency	Cumulative Percent
Active	140	50.00	140	50.00
Placebo	140	50.00	280	100.00

All values look reasonable for these variables.

Exploring Outliers and Problematic Data Distributions

Numeric variable outliers (suspiciously extreme minimum or maximum values) may be apparent in the analysis above. But you should explore them further as demonstrated below, while also consulting with your data source and the literature to verify what are reasonable minimum and maximum values. Some variables will not meet the assumptions of statistical tests (for example, will not be normally distributed). The PROC UNIVARIATE code below will get us started with useful output for the variable FG, which is fasting blood glucose value.

```
ODS listing close;
ODS rtf file="c:/temp/TIADout.rtf";
proc univariate data=TIAD;
   var FG;
   qqplot FG/normal(mu=est sigma=est color=red l=4) square;
   run;
```

```
ODS rtf close;
ODS listing;
```

We have requested the default descriptive statistics along with a quantile-quantile (Q-Q) plot, which plots observed quantiles against quantile values predicted from a normal distribution. The hope is that the values are nearly the same, and the Q-Q line is nearly straight. The option NORMAL requests the reference line from the normal distribution with MU and SIGMA estimated from the sample mean and standard deviation. Additional options request the color red for the distribution line with line type = 4. The SQUARE option formats the plot in a square.

In this example, we see an unexpectedly high fasting glucose value of 644 in both the table and the plot. The maximum value should not be much greater than the 99th percentile value of 281.67.

Figure 8.4 A Quantile Distribution Output from PROC UNIVARIATE to Check Distribution of Numerical Variable

Quantiles (Definition 5)	
Quantile	Estimate
100% Max	664.0090
99%	281.6737
95%	238.4515
90%	215.1638
75% Q3	185.4086
50% Median	157.2447
25% Q1	126.9293
10%	97.5997
5%	78.6712
1%	57.1377
0% Min	50.1519

The value is also clearly isolated in the upper right corner of the Q-Q plot.

44 Chapter 8 / Data Exploration

Figure 8.5   A Typical Q-Q Plot to Check for Outliers

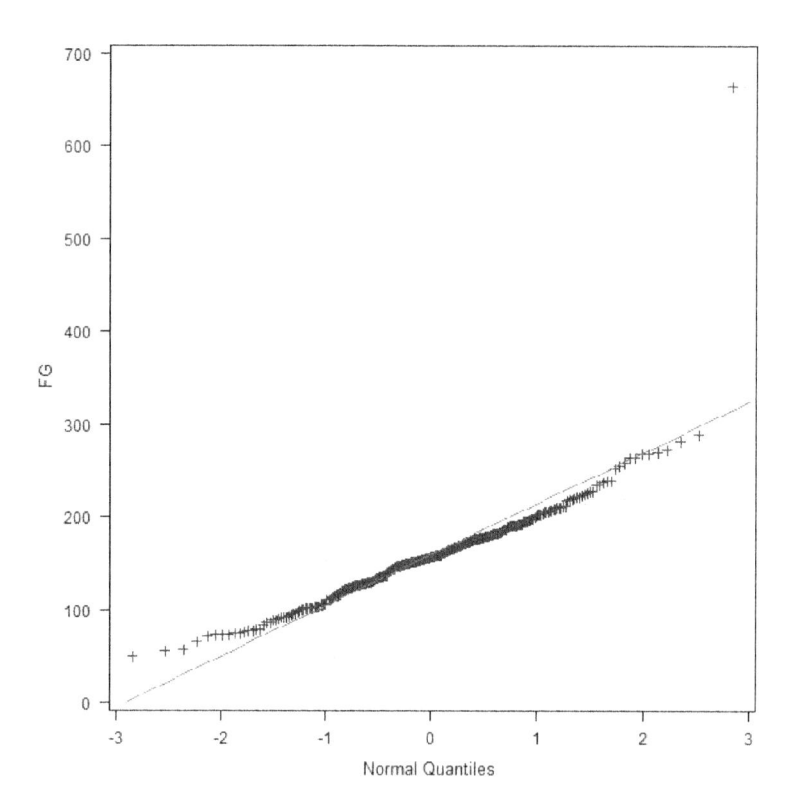

The high value prompts an inquiry to the laboratory, which reviews their data and discovers the error. The value is corrected, and the new quantile distribution and plot are presented again.

Figure 8.6 A Quantile Distribution Showing That Values Are Reasonable

Quantiles (Definition 5)	
Quantile	Estimate
100% Max	296.5499
99%	281.6737
95%	238.4515
90%	215.1638
75% Q3	185.4086
50% Median	157.2447
25% Q1	126.9293
10%	97.5997
5%	78.6712
1%	57.1377
0% Min	50.1519

46 *Chapter 8 / Data Exploration*

Figure 8.7 *A Q-Q Plot Showing That FG Has a Fairly Normal Distribution*

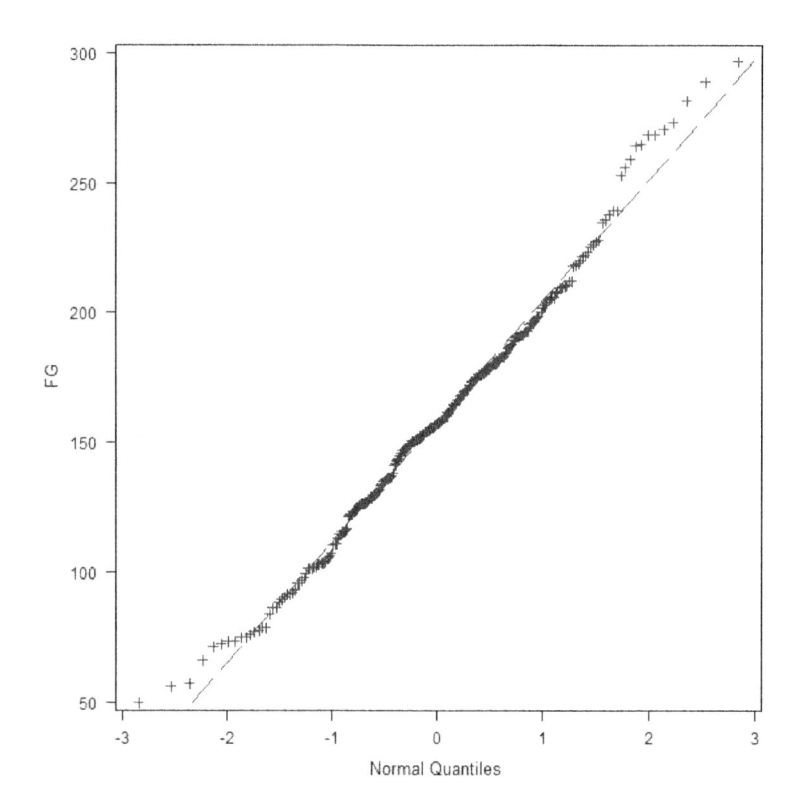

Our analysis policies require that we document in the analysis plan that an outlier was found and corrected, and that we include the revealing tables and plots. Your group's policy may not require reporting, or may only require a sentence or two that summarizes what took place.

Distribution Problems

We ran the previous PROC UNIVARIATE code for blood triglyceride level and obtained the following tables and plot as part of the output.

Figure 8.8 PROC UNIVARIATE Output Showing Skewness

Moments			
N	279	Sum Weights	279
Mean	166.362007	Sum Observations	46415
Std Deviation	84.9298576	Variance	7213.08071
Skewness	1.87201419	Kurtosis	5.20521702
Uncorrected SS	9726929	Corrected SS	2005236.44
Coeff Variation	51.051234	Std Error Mean	5.08461757

Figure 8.9 PROC UNIVARIATE Output Showing Mean and Median

Basic Statistical Measures			
Location		Variability	
Mean	166.3620	Std Deviation	84.92986
Median	147.0000	Variance	7213
Mode	119.0000	Range	560.00000
		Interquartile Range	99.00000

Figure 8.10 A Q-Q Plot Demonstrating a Skewed Distribution

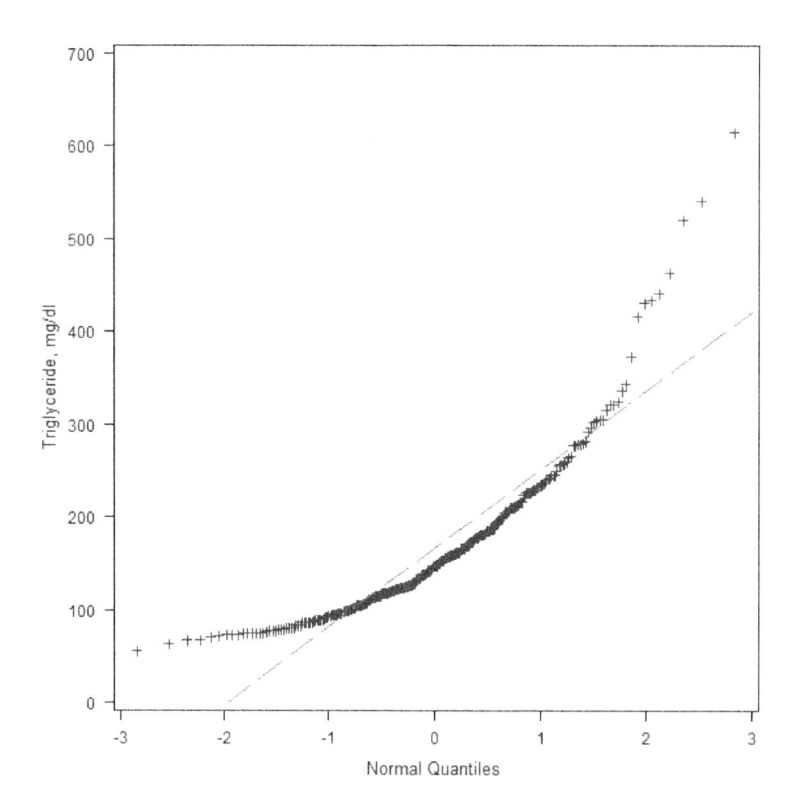

It is clear that the distribution is not normally distributed as required by the analyses we have in mind later. Three details tell you this: 1) The skewness value of 1.9 is much higher than the 0.0 value of a normal distribution; 2) the mean and the median are not equal; and 3) the quantile-quantile plot is curved instead of linear. In a quick review of the literature, or perhaps in discussion with the study team, you learn that triglyceride values are not expected to be normally distributed in any given population. Logging triglyceride is an acceptable adjustment. After this adjustment is performed, the Q-Q plot of the log of triglyceride is reasonably linear (although the tails are a bit worrisome), and a normal distribution is assumed.

Figure 8.11 A Q-Q Plot of a Transformed Variable Showing That the Transformed Variable Is Normally Distributed

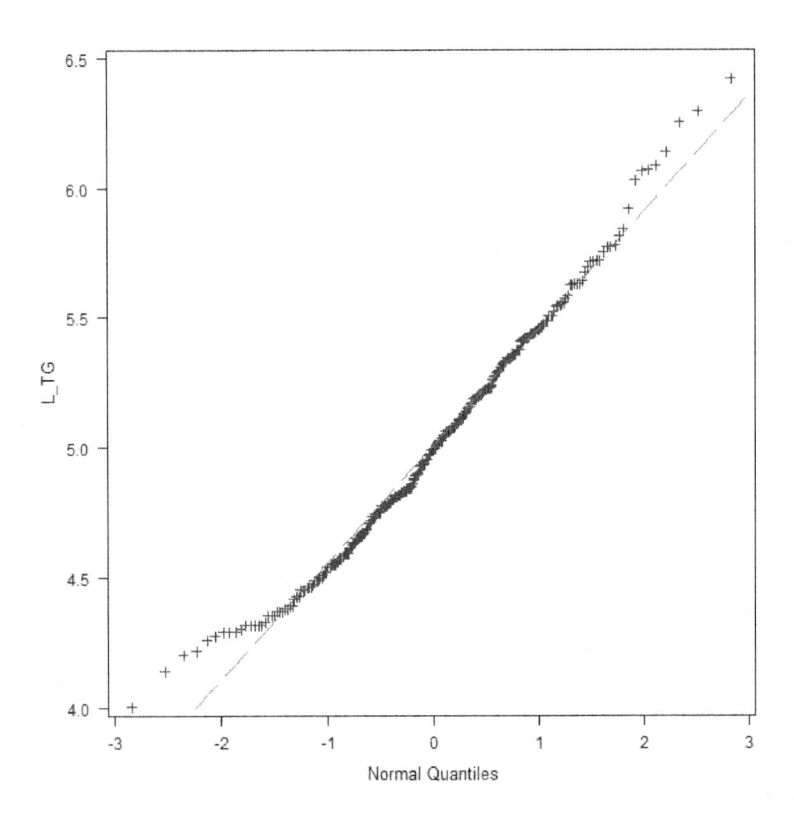

Determining the Source of Variability

The statistical analyses that you have in mind for testing the main hypotheses may require you to explore the cause of variability in certain measurements. SAS offers procedures for discovering the sources of variability for an outcome. Continuing with our clinical study example, we would like to know if patient weight significantly varies among the 12 clinics participating in the TIAD project. You would expect similar distributions in weight across clinics because the study entry criteria have beginning weight requirements. However, you have learned that some of the clinics did not train staff well enough to follow the study

50 *Chapter 8 / Data Exploration*

protocol where weight measurement was concerned. A box plot for weight by clinic shows the distribution of weight among clinics.

```
proc sort data = TIAD;
 by clinic;
 run;

ODS listing close;
ODS rtf file="c:/temp/TIADvar.rtf";
proc sgplot data = TIAD;
 vbox weight/category=clinic;
run;
ODS rtf close;
ODS listing;
```

Figure 8.12 Graph Showing Variability in Patient Weight among Clinics

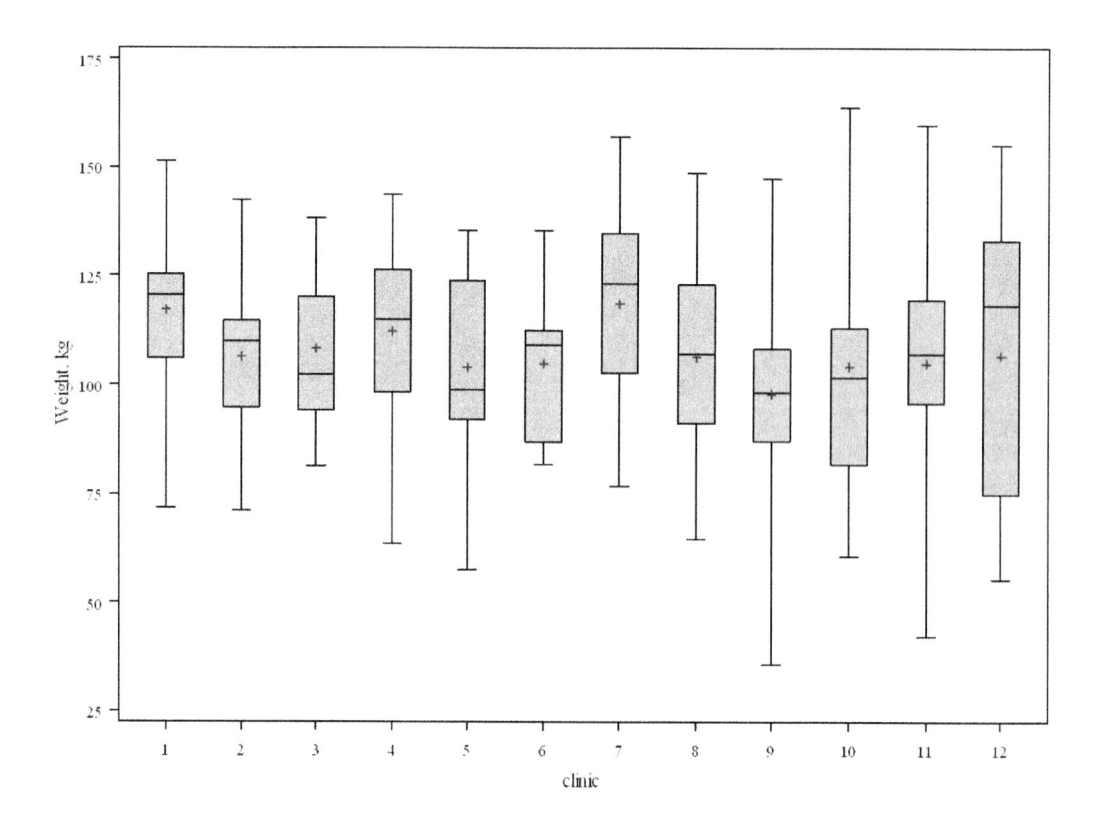

The variation among clinics looks high whether we focus on the full ranges (vertical extents), interquartile ranges (blue boxes), the medians (horizontal lines), or means (plus marks). To ensure that our eyes are not leading us astray, we will test the hypothesis of equal means and variances among clinics using the GLM procedure with the MEANS statement to compute a one-way ANOVA for weight.

```
ODS listing close;
ODS rtf file="c:/temp/TIADvar.rtf";
ODS graphics on;
   proc glm data= TIAD plot=diagnostics;
      class site;
      model weight = site;
      means site/hovtest welch;
   run;
ODS graphics off;
ODS rtf close;
ODS listing;
```

The HOVTEST option on the MEANS statement requests that Lavene's test for equal clinic variances be performed. The WELCH option, used when the HOVTEST shows unequal variances, will test for equal means in the presence of unequal group variances, which we expect to be the case based on the box plots.

If you assume an alpha of 0.05, the second table below confirms the hypothesis of unequal variances among the clinics (P <0.01). After you correct for unequal variance (Welch's adjustment), the test for differences in means is also significant as shown in the third table below (P <0.03).

Figure 8.13 PROC GLM Output Showing Variability in Weight by Clinic

Source	DF	Type III SS	Mean Square	F Value	Pr > F
clinic	11	10405.43669	945.94879	1.80	0.0547

Levene's Test for Homogeneity of Weight Variance
ANOVA of Squared Deviations from Group Means

Source	DF	Sum of Squares	Mean Square	F Value	Pr > F
clinic	11	15133925	1375811	2.98	0.0009
Error	268	1.2382E8	462009		

Welch's ANOVA for Weight

Source	DF	F Value	Pr > F
clinic	11.0000	2.16	0.0239
Error	86.0592		

Although Levene's test for homogeneity of variance is good practice, it is not a definitive test and should be backed up with additional exploration. The graphical output shown below is useful for determining whether the data will meet the assumption of equal variance in a GLM analysis.

The plot=diagnostics option of the PROC GLM statement above produces a very useful panel of diagnostic plots.

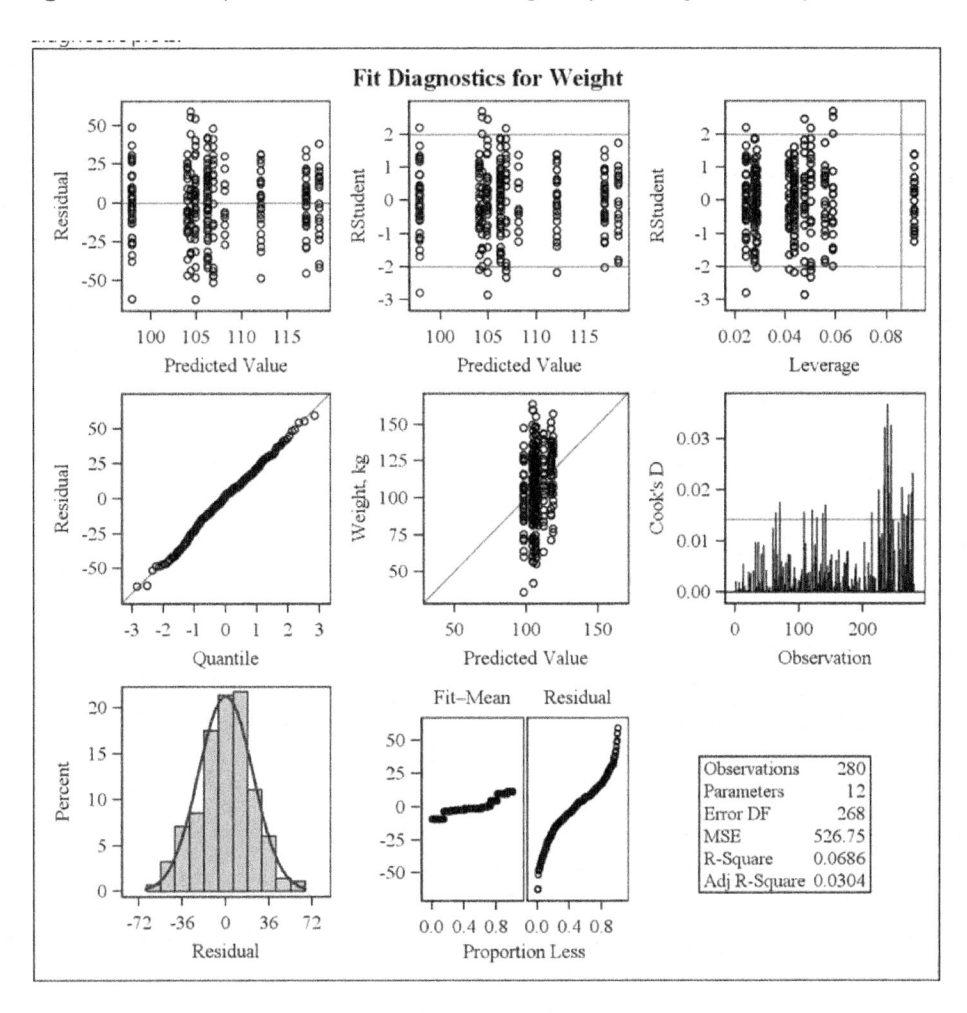

Figure 8.14 Output from PROC GLM Using the plot=diagnostics Option

The Q-Q plot of residuals (second row, first plot) is straight and indicates a good model fit. However, the spread shown in the plot of residuals versus predicted values (first row, first plot) suggests some problems. The plots of the studentized residuals (first row, second and third plots) show a number of observations outside the ± 2 range that need to be investigated. The Cook's D plot (second row, third plot) also indicates some problematic cases.

It is clear that we need to follow up with the clinics to find out why there is variation and what can be done about it before we decide how to test a hypothesis involving weight. After querying the clinics, we discover that some clinics were using a different type of scale to weigh study participants. To see if scale type is a factor, we use the variable *scale* to group the patients accordingly. We then run PROC GLM but test only for a scale effect.

```
ODS listing close;
ODS rtf file="c:/temp/TIADvar.rtf";
```

54 Chapter 8 / Data Exploration

```
ODS graphics on;
proc glm data=TIAD plot=diagnostics;
      class scale;
      model weight = scale;
      means scale/hovtest welch;
   run;
ODS graphics off;
ODS rtf close;
ODS listing;
```

Figure 8.15 *Output from PROC GLM with plot=diagnostics Option Showing Variation by Scale Type*

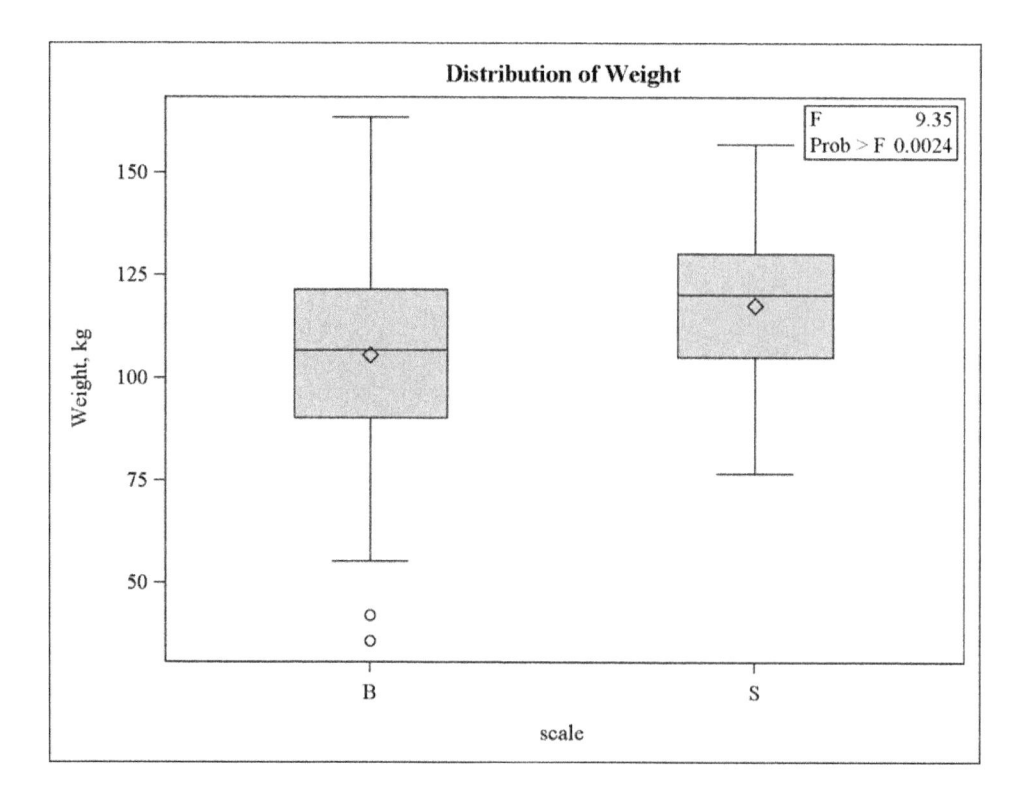

The diagnostics plots from a GLM analysis of clinic and scale type (simultaneously, not shown) indicate that there are still outliers and differences in weight between clinics even after adjusting for scale type. In our plan to test hypotheses that specify weight as an outcome, we will have to account for this unexpected source of variation and perhaps propose an alternative to an ordinary least squares model such as robust regression, which weights outlying data in a way that minimizes its impact on the model fit.

Producing Baseline Tables

Depending on how much data you have in hand while writing the analysis plan, you may want to produce a baseline table to summarize the unit of analysis for discussion with the project team. Sometimes questions have to be modified because of lack of sample size. A baseline table can help decide this.

SAS provides several ways to produce tables. You may elect to use PROC FREQ and PROC MEANS, creating tables using ODS, placing them in a Word document, and modifying them. But SAS also provides two powerful tools to output tables with minimal intervention on your part: PROC TABULATE and PROC REPORT. PROC TABULATE can be used to create tabular reports with descriptive information, so it is ideal for producing a baseline table. PROC REPORT is more flexible, combining the features of PROC PRINT, PROC MEANS, and PROC TABULATE, allowing cumulative row and column totals.

Before you attempt to produce a table, decide how you would like the table to look, and perhaps create a shell table in Microsoft Excel or Word. Specify the classification variables and the analysis variables, define the dimensions of the table, and identify the statistics you would like to include.

The code and output we obtained with PROC TABULATE for our TIAD study is shown below.

```
proc format;
  value tx_  0 = 'Active'
             1 = 'Placebo';
  value sex_ 1 = 'Male'
             2 = 'Female';
         run;

ODS listing close;
ODS rtf file="c:/temp/TIADbase.rtf";
proc tabulate data = tiad;
 class tx sex;
 var age bmi hba1c glucose;
 table (age bmi hba1c glucose), tx*(n mean std);
 table sex, tx*(n pctn);
 format tx tx_. sex sex_.;
 run;
ODS rtf close;
ODS listing;
```

Figure 8.16 Tables Showing PROC TABULATE Output

	Treatment Group					
	Active			Placebo		
	N	Mean	Std	N	Mean	Std
Age at randomization, y	140	46.30	9.29	140	46.21	9.13
BMI, kg/m2	140	33.76	8.52	140	33.05	7.88
HbA1c, mg/dl	109	8.11	0.79	109	8.05	0.75
Glucose, mg/dl	109	143.79	37.71	109	138.39	35.90

	Treatment Group			
	Active		Placebo	
	N	PctN	N	PctN
Sex				
Male	79	28.21	74	26.43
Female	61	21.79	66	23.57

Although two tables are created, one for continuous variables and one for categorical, it is not difficult to combine them into one table if you prefer. You could use a word processor and change the headings to reflect the mix of statistics in some columns ("Pct or Mean").

Figure 8.17 A Microsoft Word Table Combining the PROC TABULATE Output

| | Treatment Group ||||||
| | Active ||| Placebo |||
	N	Pct or Mean	Std	N	Pct or Mean	Std
Sex						
Male	79	28.21		74	26.43	
Female	61	21.79	9.29	66	23.57	9.13
Age at randomization, y	140	46.30	9.29	140	46.21	9.13
BMI, kg/m²	140	33.76	8.52	140	33.05	7.88
HbA1c, mg/dl	109	8.11	0.79	109	8.05	0.75
Glucose, mg/dl	109	143.79	37.71	109	138.39	35.90

You will want to discuss the baseline table with the project team. In our case, the team needs to be aware of the missing data for HbA1c and Glucose. Why are there 140 cases but only 109 values for these two variables? If the problem cannot be corrected, this will change power estimates that were previously calculated.

Communicating with the Project Team

When this section of the analysis plan has been drafted, you should have a good feel for the data. All of this information should be discussed with the project team as appropriate. They should be aware of problems with missing data, variable distributions, and other information that may affect the conclusions that can be made from the data.

Analysis

Summary	59
General Approach	60
Statistical Parameters	60
Missing Values	62
Results Reporting	63
Analysis of Questions/Hypotheses	63
Primary Hypotheses	63
Secondary Hypotheses	69
References	69

Summary

The first section of this chapter discusses the part of the data analysis plan in which all parameters and assumptions you anticipate using throughout the rest of the analysis are presented. Much of the information in this section may be pulled from the analysis policies document. Parts of this section can be used in the methods section of the final report.

Next is a section covering analytic methods that will be applied to specific questions or hypotheses. The sections should be repeated for each question or hypothesis. If there will be primary and secondary analyses, it may be wise to organize the question sections into those two divisions.

General Approach

Statistical Parameters

Note that if two or more comparisons are planned, there are two kinds of type I errors: experiment-wise and comparison-wise error rates. The experiment-wise error rate is the probability of making at least one type I error when testing a whole collection of comparisons. The comparison-wise error rate is the probability of a type I error set by the analyst for evaluating each comparison.

State the type I error rate or level of significance (alpha-level) to be used for all analysis and whether statistical tests will be one- or two-sided. An example might be "All tests will be two-sided and considered statistically significant if $P<0.05$".

Describe how you will adjust the level of significance when testing multiple hypotheses. Suppose, for example, you plan to carry out five independent hypothesis tests at the 0.05 alpha-level. You may recall from statistics training that the probability of declaring any one of the tests significant under the null hypothesis is 0.05, but the experiment-wise error rate–the probability of declaring at least one of the five tests (number of comparisons, nc in the formula below) significant due to chance alone–is much higher and computed as follows.

P(one significant result) = 1-P(no significant results)

= $1-(1-alpha)^{nc}$

= $1-(1-0.05)^{5}$

= 0.226

Thus with five tests, there is a 23% chance of observing at least one significant result even if in the real world all five tested relationships are not real. Therefore, you will have to adjust the level of significance for individual tests in order to keep the probability of observing at least one significant result due to chance below your desired significance level.

You should state how you are going to do this. The classic Bonferroni adjustment, which divides your chosen alpha by the number of tests, is available in a number of SAS procedures such as PROC GLM and PROC ANOVA. However, it is widely recognized to be overly conservative and results in false negative findings. PROC GLM offers several other options for multiple comparison adjustment such as Tukey-Kramer (TUKEY), Dunnett (DUNNETT), Sidak (SIDAK) among others.

PROC MULTTEST offers some elegant and less conservative *p*-value adjustment methods, including several step-down, step-up, bootstrap, and permutation methods. PROC MULTTEST can run statistical analyses directly on raw data or can accept as input the *p*-values output by other procedures. State in your plan which route you intend to take.

You should plan to explain these matters to your investigative team before you conduct actual analyses. Therefore, you might include a hypothetical example of what the raw and adjusted *p*-values could look like to prepare for the discussion. An example is given below.

```
data mytests;
 input testnum raw_p;
datalines;
1 0.0075
2 0.0369
3 0.0412
4 0.0782
5 0.0123
;
Run;
ODS listing close;
ODS rtf file="c:\temp\TIADpval.rtf";
proc multtest inpvalues=mytests holm;
run;
ODS rtf close;
ODS listing;
```

Here we have read in the *p*-value results of a family of five hypothesis tests that were conducted for our fictional TIAD study. We have specified the HOLM option, which requests that a step-down Bonferroni adjustment be applied to the original *p*-values.

Figure 9.1 Output of PROC MULTITEST Showing p-Value Adjustment

P-Value Adjustment Information	
P-Value Adjustment	Stepdown Bonferroni

p-Values		
Test	Raw	Stepdown Bonferroni
1	0.0075	0.0375
2	0.0369	0.1107
3	0.0412	0.1107
4	0.0782	0.1107
5	0.0123	0.0492

Depending on the statistical knowledge of your co-investigators, they might be grumpy and may even push back when you inform them that the unadjusted *p*-value for hypotheses 2 and 3 were statistically significant at the unadjusted alpha-level of 0.05 but not at the adjusted value of 0.111. This is a good time to discuss with them what "statistically significant" means and how to interpret *p*-values.

Missing Values

Missing data should be explored to be sure there is no bias introduced by the missing values. PROC MEANS with the NMISS option provides a quick way to discover the number of missing values in your data.

```
proc means data = TIAD nmiss;
 var HbA1c Glucose Age;
run;
```

If you have missing values, then explain in your plan how they will be handled in the analysis. Sometimes missing data can simply be ignored if analysis or other information at your disposal indicates that the missingness is unbiased or random. However, missing data may also be imputed. If missing data is to be imputed, you must state exactly which of the many methods available will be used, and how you plan to account for the missing data with uncertainty using multiple imputation methods to adjust for standard error.

As an alternative to imputing missing values, there are statistical models that can account for missing data such as those that use maximum likelihood estimates (MLE). Missing values are not imputed per se. Instead, all available data is used to compute the MLE. These methods are available in the MI, MIXED, and GLIMMIX procedures. A good source for learning these methods is "Multiple Imputation of Missing Data Using SAS" (Berglund and Heeringa 2014).

It may also be necessary to perform a sensitivity analysis showing how the results respond under different assumptions about missingness. For example, you may analyze the data using the assumption that all of the missing values would have been clinically negative (e.g., in the normal blood glucose range).

Results Reporting

State how you intend to report analysis results. This may entail only one or two sentences taken directly from your analysis policy. For example, you may state that you will report the statistical estimate of each analysis along with its 95% confidence intervals.

Analysis of Questions/Hypotheses

Primary Hypotheses

State the Hypothesis

State each null hypothesis and its alternative hypothesis in words. Also, give the formal statistical statement of the hypothesis, because it might be useful for a statistical reviewer to see in the final report or manuscript. For example, we might test the null hypothesis of no difference between two groups of patients in mean Hba1c, a type of hemoglobin that is elevated in diabetics, against the alternative hypothesis that a difference will be found.

$H_o : \mu_1 = \mu_2$

$H_A : \mu_1 \neq \mu_2$

where, μ_1 =mean HbaA1c in the active treatment group and μ_2 =mean HbaA1c in the placebo group.

Analysis

In this section, state the statistical methods you will use to test the hypotheses (e.g., t-test, analysis of variance, simple linear regression, etc.). If multiple methods will be used, make it clear which method will be used for which hypothesis. List the assumptions for each method (e.g., equal sample variances for t-tests). List all covariates that will be used in any given analysis. Finally, define any subsequent analyses that may be done, such as pre-specified subgroup analysis or sensitivity analysis.

Sample Size and Power

It almost goes without saying that your study should have sufficient sample size and statistical power to make a meaningful conclusion. Power is the probability of rejecting the null hypothesis when the alternative is true. You want to be sure to have enough power so that the probability of rejecting the null hypothesis when the alternative is true is high. Most studies set power at 80%.

In clinical studies and under most other circumstances, it is important that your analysis plan covers sample size and statistical power, particularly for the primary hypothesis, but often for analyses of secondary questions as well. Sample size and power calculations are not only helpful for study planning, but they may also be helpful in interpreting negative findings.

Statistical reviewers of reports and manuscripts sometimes ask for these calculations long after the original analysis has been conducted. Alas, such post hoc power analysis is not useful (Goodman and Berlin, 1994), so it is better to have thought through sample size and power before conducting the statistical analysis. If you are working on a funded project, it may be the case that sample size and power calculations were performed for the grant or contract proposal. But even in these cases, the assumptions that went into these calculations may have changed, necessitating a re-do of the calculations. In other situations, the sample size and power calculations have never been done, and presenting them in the analysis plan is a good idea.

Most often, sample size is calculated for a primary hypothesis. In your sample size discussion, you should state the following:

- the null hypothesis and the alternative
- α, the probability of making a type 1 error (significance or alpha level)
- β, the probability of making a type 2 error and therefore power (1-β)
- the statistical test upon which the calculation is based
- estimates of the parameters being tested—for example, means and standard deviations (these may come from estimates available in the published literature)
- estimates of the difference or effect size that the study is powered to detect (choose the smallest effect size that would produce a meaningful or useful effect in the real world)

For example, for the TIAD study, we are interested in testing the null hypothesis of no difference in mean HbA1c between the active drug treatment group and the placebo group. After discussions with the study team, statistical test parameters were chosen, and sample estimates were selected, informed by a literature review. PROC POWER was used to calculate appropriate sample sizes. The code and results are shown below.

```
proc power;
 twosamplemeans
 test=diff
 groupmeans=7.8 | 7.2
 stddev=1
 alpha=0.05
 nperg=.
 power=.80;
run;
```

The TWOSAMPLEMEANS statement is appropriate for our situation. The TEST=DIFF option tests for a simple difference in means under the assumption of equal sample variances. With the GROUPMEANS option, we specify the expected effects based on our literature review (treatment group mean listed second). With the NPERG=. and POWER=.80 options, we have requested a solution for the equivalent sample sizes that would be needed to achieve the desired power of 80% under the stated circumstances.

The output below indicates that we need at least 45 cases in each group to achieve our desired power. Hopefully, this analysis was done before the study was funded and the data was collected.

Figure 9.2 Output of PROC POWER for a Two-Sample t Test

The POWER Procedure
Two-Sample t Test for Mean Difference

Fixed Scenario Elements	
Distribution	Normal
Method	Exact
Alpha	0.05
Group 1 Mean	7.8
Group 2 Mean	7.2
Standard Deviation	1
Nominal Power	0.8
Number of Sides	2
Null Difference	0

Computed N Per Group	
Actual Power	N Per Group
0.804	45

In writing your analysis plan, introduce the section on power analysis with a discussion of what would be considered a meaningful difference in group outcomes based on the literature. In our case, we would explain why a difference between 7.8 and 7.2 in HbA1c is clinically significant. You will already have stated your null and alternative hypotheses. Here is some language to describe the results of the power analysis:

With a desired significance level of 5% and power of 80%, we will need 45 subjects per group in order to conduct a two-sided t-test of a difference in mean HbA1c, given that a clinically significant reduction in HbA1c is the value of 0.6 (or greater). These calculations assumed a mean HbA1c measurement in the placebo group of 7.8% and 7.2% in the active arm with equal variance of 1 in both groups.

For secondary analysis studies, very often the sample size is already set. The best you can do is estimate the power of the planned analysis and hope it is sufficient. Under these circumstances you will state sample size and request output of the power value. For example, suppose we have 80 patients per group from a prior study. Our PROC POWER statements would be as follows:

```
proc power;
  twosamplemeans
  test=diff
  groupmeans=7.8 | 7.2
  stddev=1
  alpha=0.05
  nperg=80
  power=.;
run;
```

Note the changes in the NPERG and POWER options in this scenario. The output shows us that we have a very healthy 97% power to detect a difference in means, given the stated assumptions.

Figure 9.3 A Power Estimate Using PROC POWER

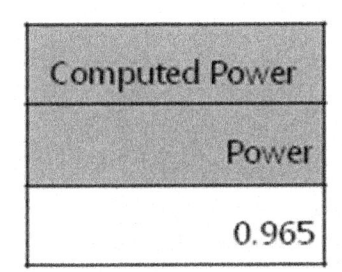

Computed Power
Power
0.965

Covariates

Covariates are variables that may not be of direct interest in your study, but are highly correlated with your outcome measure. Hence, you may make incorrect conclusions if known or suspected covariates are not adjusted for in your analyses. Many statistical methods allow for covariate adjustments. Confounding variables are a type of covariate that is associated with both the exposure (treatment) variable and the outcome variable (but is not in the causal pathway between exposure and outcome). Identification of covariates and confounders *before* an analysis and planning for their inclusion in your analyses is critical, because missing them can lead to erroneous results.

A common assumption for statistical models is independence among covariates. However, you should plan to test covariates for collinearity (excessive intercorrelation). If it exists, it can result in unreliable interpretation of the effect of individual independent (predictor) variables on the outcome.

Although you may not actually conduct the collinearity analysis in the planning stage, you should, at the very least, state how you plan to go about it. For example, PROC REG includes collinearity diagnostics. Your primary analysis may not be regression, but you can still take advantage of the PROC REG collinearity diagnostics, because only the relationships among the covariates are analyzed. The diagnostics include testing for variance inflation factors (VIF), tolerance (TOL), and condition indices (COLLIN and COLLINOINT).

Below is a demonstration of a test for collinearity among three predictor variables – weight, height and BMI – that we anticipate using as covariates in our TIAD study. Note that the dependent variable tg is not of interest—we are only using it to get the collinearity diagnostics out of PROC REG.

```
ODS listing close;
ODS rtf file="c:/temp/TIADcoll.rtf";
proc reg data = TIAD;
 model tg = weight height bmi /collinoint;
 run;
ODS rtf close;
ODS listing;
```

The COLLINOINT option excludes the intercept in the calculation of the collinearity statistics because it is not of interest.

Figure 9.4 *Output of PROC REG with COLLINOINT Option Showing the Condition Index*

		Collinearity Diagnostics (intercept adjusted)			
Number	Eigenvalue	Condition Index	Weight	Height	bmi
1	1.90000	1.00000	0.00543	0.00229	0.00568
2	1.09011	1.32021	0.00411	0.05413	0.00011480
3	0.00989	13.86362	0.99046	0.94358	0.99420

The table is comparable to a principal components analysis of the correlation matrix of the three variables. It is beyond the scope of this book to explain principal components analysis. The analysis output by PROC REG creates components (table rows) equal to the number of input variables, and the rows are sorted in descending order on something called a condition index. Condition indices of 10 or more may indicate that there is some degree of correlation among at least two input variables (Belsley, Kuh, and Welsch, 2004).

The condition index for component number 3 above is higher than 10, which may indicate at least a weak correlation among the variables and may affect the regression estimates. The values in the proportion of variation columns indicate how strongly each variable "loads on" (i.e., is correlated with) each component. We see that all three variables are heavily loaded on component 3. In essence, the analysis has discovered a principal component in the data that explains a great deal of the variation in all three variables. Or stated another way, all three variables vary in unison.

This is not surprising, considering that weight and height are related in nature, and BMI is calculated directly from them. These three variables should not be used together in a regression model. Removing height from the analysis produces a component table of two rows (not shown), and no condition indices greater than 10. We conclude that weight and BMI can be entered into a model together. Note that it is common for there to be some correlation between covariates.

Subgroup Analysis and Sensitivity Analysis

Define any further analysis that will be done such as pre-specified subgroup analysis or sensitivity analyses.

Secondary Hypotheses

For each additional hypothesis, list the null and alternative hypothesis and the analysis method that will be used to test the null. State the assumptions and define any further analysis that might be done.

References

Belsley, David A, and Edwin Kuh, Roy E. Welsch. *Regression Diagnostics: Identifying Influential Data and Sources of Collinearity*. Hoboken, NJ: John Wiley and Sons, Inc. 2004.

Berglund, Patricia, and Steven Heeringa. *Multiple Imputation of Missing Data Using SAS®*. Cary, NC: SAS Institute Inc. 2014.

Goodman, Steven N. and Jesse A. Berlin. "The Use of Predicted Confidence Intervals When Planning Experiments and the Misuse of Power When Interpreting Results." *Ann Intern Med* 122 (6)1994: 200-206.

10

Potential Conclusions, Study Weaknesses, and a Timeline

Summary 71
Potential Conclusions 71
Limitations and Weaknesses 72
Timeline 72

Summary

This chapter encourages the analyst to outline the possible conclusions, limitations, and weaknesses of the investigation and the schedule for analytical work. Stating these before analysis takes place can help to rein in expectations about the study results.

Potential Conclusions

State the conclusions that you hope to gain from doing the study. State the population to which the results apply. Explain how each conclusion may advance or reframe the literature on the subject matter, and in the case of clinical or public health studies, how the results might inform healthcare delivery or policy. Indicate what future research might be done once the study is completed and outline some follow-up activities. This section might be a restatement of earlier sections of the analysis plan, but it keeps the study team engaged and excited about the potentially far-reaching effects of the project.

Limitations and Weaknesses

Summarize the limitations and weaknesses of the study. Some examples of limitations include a limited sample size or lack of reliable data such as self-reported data, missing data, and deficiencies in data measurements (such as a questionnaire item not asked that could have been used to address a specific issue). Assess the impact of these on the interpretation of the results. Indicate how future research studies might avoid these limitations and weaknesses. As analysis progresses, other limitations and weaknesses may become apparent and should be added to this section of the analysis plan. For example, a variable may not have been measured in the way you originally thought. Instead of gleaning the diagnosis of a disease from a chart, the patient was asked if a doctor had ever diagnosed them with a certain disease. A self-reported diagnosis usually does not carry the same meaning as a diagnosis extracted from a chart.

You may also want to add a paragraph on future directions. This research may be the first step in what the research group hopes will be a series of studies. An observational study using archived data may be planned for this research, but the research group views this as a preliminary study used for planning an experimental study. Stating this is helpful to keep everyone focused on the long term goal.

Timeline

Just as in grant applications, it is helpful in an analysis plan to include a timeline to let the study team know when activities are likely to begin and end. Be realistic about the schedule. A simple Gantt chart should suffice. Templates are available for Microsoft Excel, but SAS PROC GANTT is also suitable and provides a great deal of flexibility for more complex tasks. Include key tasks that should be carried out prior to conducting the main analysis such as data cleaning. Propose beginning and end dates for each task. Include time for communicating and evaluating each task with the study team. The data analyst is usually responsible for keeping to the timeline, so be prepared to make quick adjustments to the schedule as they become necessary and circulate the new schedule promptly.

Revising, Producing and Sharing the Plan

Summary 73
Communicating and Revising the Plan 73
Turning the Plan into a Report 74
Developing Tabular Presentations 74
Cross-References 75
Unplanned Analysis 75
Closing Remarks 76

Summary

Communication is the key to conducting a scientifically solid, reproducible study. This chapter discusses the importance of communicating with the study team, obtaining feedback, and updating the plan. We also provide tips for producing the plan document.

Communicating and Revising the Plan

Review the plan with the study team. As discussions proceed, modifications to the plan will probably be necessary. It is very useful to have a section at the beginning of the document that records revision events. Each event (row) might have the date of modification, summary and section of the modification, reason for the change, and perhaps the parties responsible for the change. Major revisions should be reviewed and approved by the study team to ensure that you understood and translated them correctly.

Turning the Plan into a Report

As you developed the plan, you discussed each step with the research team and updated the plan with new information. As you begin to test each hypothesis, you should continue to update the plan with results. In this way, the plan morphs into a results document or final report. As this happens, you should document any problems that were encountered and the decisions, actions, or methods you used to overcome these problems. The beauty of developing the plan in this way is that it becomes a results-laden document that is easily tweaked into a report or a manuscript. However, the most compelling reason to develop it into a results document is that each step is documented well enough that the entire project is reproducible and hence more defensible.

Developing Tabular Presentations

We recommend using the SAS Output Delivery System (ODS) to produce RTF-formatted tables. These can be easily inserted directly into your word processor's final report, presentation, or manuscript.

For long tables or in situations in which you must produce many tables, you may prefer to transmit an Excel workbook to your audience as an appendix or supplement to your main report. To accomplish this, use the ODS statement TAGSETS.EXECLXP to write results directly into multiple worksheets in a single Excel workbook.

With the code below, we create an Excel workbook with a separate worksheet for each country. This is accomplished with the SHEET_INTERVAL option and the use of variable country for BY processing in the PROC TABLULATE.

```
ods listing close;
ods tagsets.excelxp file='c:\temp\TIADexample.xls' style=statistical
       options( sheet_interval='bygroup' );
run;

proc tabulate data = tiad;
 class tx sex;
 var age bmi hba1c glucose;
 table (age bmi hba1c glucose), tx*(n mean std);
 table sex, tx*(n pctn);
 format tx tx_. sex sex_.;
 by country;
```

```
  run;
ods tagsets.excelxp close;
ods listing;
```

Cross-References

In your SAS programs, insert comments that cross reference sections of the analysis plan. This is just another way to ensure that all of your steps are documented. And it makes it very easy to adapt both your plan and SAS programs to similar projects months or years later. Number your comments to correspond to each section of the analysis plan. Insert each comment at the beginning of the relevant section of your code. In the case of long programs that address multiple sections of the plan, consider listing all of the cross-referencing comments in the header of the program for easy lookup.

For example, Section 4 of the TIAD Study presents data tables and variable definitions. Part A in Section 4 presents a mockup of a baseline table. The distribution of each variable will be analyzed before populating the table with data. Therefore, in your SAS program, you identify this topic accordingly.

```
*-----------------------------------------------------------*;
*--- 4A. Baseline Characteristics Distribution Analysis *;
*-----------------------------------------------------------*;
```

If you need to update the data table showing baseline characteristics, you will be able to find the code quickly.

Unplanned Analysis

Among the many advantages of writing an analysis plan is that you will be able to use it to limit investigations that otherwise may have a tendency to drift away from the primary question. It is normal for a client to start asking additional questions before the first one is answered. In order to keep the focus on the proposed topics, the team should avoid tangents. Otherwise, time and resources will be wasted. One way to lend an ear to these additional questions without acting on them in the current effort is to add a section titled "Future Directions." It may be empty out the outset, but your team members will remember it was there and can recall its purpose when new ideas occur. Summarize all new questions or hypotheses here, to be saved for another study.

In other cases, it may actually be deemed necessary to carry out analyses that were not in the original plan. These may be due to an outside event such as the publication of a report that impacts the questions and therefore the direction of the current investigation. Amend the plan accordingly, document the reasons for the changes, and update sections as necessary. And, as always, review the plan with the investigative team.

Closing Remarks

This book has taken you through the stages of conceiving, developing, and implementing an analysis plan. The ideas presented in this book can be applied to any field of investigation although it may be necessary to modify the stages of planning in terms of timing, data processing, and statistical analyses to make them more appropriate for your field.

However, we recommend against compromising your analysis policies or any of the mathematical assumptions that underlie the statistical methods and interpretations that are best for your situation. We know from decades of experience that analysts sometimes face enormous pressure to deviate from a rational plan or even avoid the planning stage entirely in order to satisfy the vision or schedule of senior colleagues, powerful administrators, or important clients. It is particularly shocking to recently graduated analysts who are coerced to ignore the mathematics, statistics, and scientific principles gained in the classroom. We hope this book can serve as a backstop in those situations.

We also encourage you to expand or improve on what has been presented here. For example, SAS Enterprise Guide and SAS Studio are two relatively new products that greatly facilitate the organization of data files, processing, analysis, and reporting tasks. They also make many of the features of SAS more accessible to beginners and demonstrable to colleagues and clients.

Finally, we encourage all readers to provide comments and suggestions that will improve the information and materials presented here.

12

Example Analysis Plan: The TIAD Study

Summary	78
Introduction	78
Questions	79
Primary Outcome	79
Secondary Outcomes	79
Data Description	79
Initial Data Tables and Variable Distributions	80
Baseline Characteristics	80
General Approach	82
Analysis Policy	82
Longitudinal Data Analysis	82
Analysis of Hypotheses	83
HbA1c Response	83
Change in HbA1c from Baseline to Week 48 or Last HabA1c Measured prior to Rescue Therapy	84
Change in Measurements	84

Summary

This section includes an example of an analysis plan. The plan is to analyze a fictitious drug, athelis. The plan is based on a real clinical trial, but many of the tables such as baseline and secondary outcomes, have been shortened to save space.

Introduction

The primary objective of the TIAD (**T**argeting **I**nflammation Using **A**thelis for Type 2 **D**iabetes) study is to determine whether athelis represents a new pharmacological option for diabetes management which will safely and effectively lower blood glucose levels.

TIAD is a two-stage study. The primary objective of the first stage was to select a dose of athelis that was both well-tolerated and demonstrated a trend toward improvement in glycemic control. A 3.5 g/day dose was selected, and the first stage 2 patient was screened on February 3, 2014. This analysis plan is for stage 2 and will be submitted to the data safety monitoring board for approval.

Table 12.1 TIAD Study Team

Name	Affiliation	Role
Gandalf Grey, M.D.	Great State University	Principal Investigator
Frodo Baggins, M.D.	Presidents Medical Center	Co-Investigator, Clinician
Arwen Evenstar, PhD	Principal Private College	Co-Investigator, Statistician
Meriadoc Brandybuck, PhD	Principal Private College	Co-Investigator, Statistician

Questions

Primary Outcome

The primary outcome for the TIAD study is change in HbA1c blood level from baseline to week 48 in the intent-to-treat (ITT) population. The best long-term indicator of blood glucose levels is HbA1c (glycated hemoglobin). If athelis is found to significantly lower HbA1c blood levels, clinicians will have a new option for treating this disease. The 48-week duration for the trial was chosen in order to assess both safety and efficacy.

Secondary Outcomes

Important secondary outcomes are listed below. These are outcomes of interest in monitoring the metabolic health of patients with type 2 diabetes.

- Change from baseline to either 48 weeks or last HbA1c measurement prior to rescue therapy
- Trends in HbA1c over time
- Changes in body weight over time
- Change from baseline and trends in fasting glucose over time
- Response rates for the following:
    - reduction in fasting glucose of ≥20 mg/dl
    - reduction in HbA1c of ≥0.5%
    - reduction in HbA1c of ≥0.8%

Data Description

Data for this study was collected under protocol v2.4, December 03, 2015. The first stage 2 patient was screened on February 03, 2014, and the last patient was randomized November 14, 2015. The last patient was seen on December 13, 2015, and the final safety visit occurred on January 12, 2016.

The figure below shows the study flow for the 358 randomized patients.

Figure 12.1 TIAD Study Flow

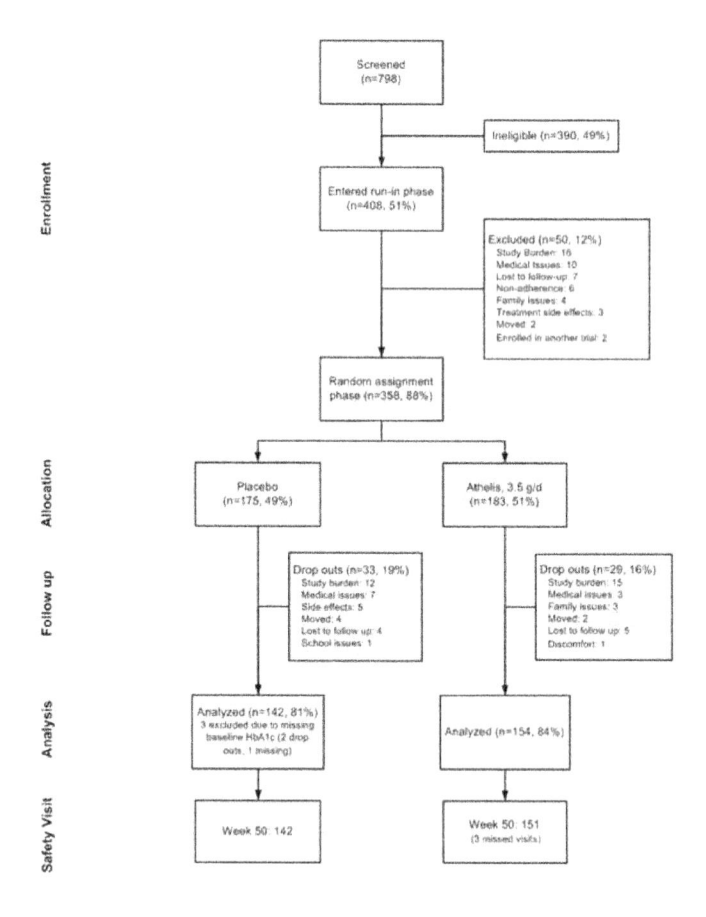

Initial Data Tables and Variable Distributions

Baseline Characteristics

The purpose of these analyses is to ensure that an equal distribution in demographic characteristics was achieved in the four treatment groups. Comparison of the baseline characteristics between the two treatment groups will use standard parametric and nonparametric statistical techniques, such as the Chi-square test and Fisher's exact test for categorical data and the t-test and Wilcoxon rank sum test for continuous data. If differences are found, the final analysis will be adjusted by the baseline characteristic as appropriate.

Table 12.2 Template for Analysis of Baseline Characteristic by Treatment Arm

Baseline Characteristic	Total (n=284)	Athelis 3.5 g (n=146)	Placebo (n=140)	P val
Age (yr)				
Female sex (% of patients)				
White race (% of patients)				
Weight (kg)				
BMI (kg/m^2)				
Waist circumference (cm)				
Time since diabetes diagnosed (yr)				
Family history* of type 1 diabetes				
Family history of type 2 diabetes				
Family history of CVD**				
Blood pressure (mm Hg)				
Systolic				
Diastolic				
Heart rate (bpm)				
Laboratory values				
Cholesterol (mg/dl)				
Triglycerides (mg/dl)				
Fasting Glucose (mg/dl)				
Age (yr)				
Female sex (% of patients)				
White race (% of patients)				

Baseline Characteristic	Total (n=284)	Athelis 3.5 g (n=146)	Placebo (n=140)	P val
Weight (kg)				
BMI (kg/m²)				
Waist circumference (cm)				

*Family history = first degree relatives

**CVD = Coronary heart disease, heart attack, stroke

General Approach

Analysis Policy

Data Analysis will adhere to the Data Analysis Policy approved by the TIAD Executive Committee on April 1, 2013.

Longitudinal Data Analysis

We will use a repeated measures, mixed model to test whether athelis changes lab and clinical measurements over time. The following model will be fit:

$Y_i = X_i + Z_i i + i$,

Where,

$Y_i = (y_{ij})'$ is a column vector of the response variable (for example, change in HbA1c from baseline) for patient i, $i = 1, ..., n$, measured at time j, $j = 0, 1, ...6$ (weeks 0, 8, 12, 16, 24, 36, and 48);

The design matrix **X** contains the fixed effects, treatments (placebo versus athelis dose 3.5) and baseline measurements; and

The design matrix **Z** contains the random effects, clinic, and time.

Under such a model, we assume that the correlation within each patient follows an autoregressive covariance pattern. This pattern assumes that the variability in measurements is constant regardless of when it was measured. It also assumes that the closer in time two values are measured, the correlation will be higher than two measurements from time points further apart in time.

- If clinic and study time explain little variation in the measurement, the terms will be dropped from the model.
- The residuals will be analyzed for model fit.
- The F-test for the overall effect of treatment group will be reported.

Analysis of Hypotheses

HbA1c Response

The primary outcome for the TIAD study is change in HbA1c level from baseline to week 48 in the intent-to-treat (ITT) population. In this analysis, we will include 283 patients, 137 in the placebo arm, and 146 in the athelis arm. Of the 286 randomized as shown in Figure 1, three HbA1c baseline results are missing in the placebo arm and must be excluded. Two were randomized but dropped out of the trial before blood was drawn. One is missing due to a lab error. The median follow-up time in both groups is 48 weeks with a minimum of 0 and a maximum of 48.

- We will use a repeated measures mixed model as described above.
- Tables 12.3 and 12.4 below show the information we will present.
- We will also analyze the change in HbA1c by treatment group adjusted for change in diabetic medications.
- The data will also be shown a figure with study time on the x axis and change in HbA1c on the y-axis for each treatment group.

Table 12.3 Change in HbA1c from Baseline by Treatment Group

Treatment Group	Mean Delta HbA1c, % (95% Confidence Limits)	P val	Mean Difference Between Treatment Groups (95% Confidence Limits)	P val
Placebo				
3.5 g				

Table 12.4 Change in HbA1c from Baseline by Treatment Group and Study Week

	Placebo		3.5g	
Study Week	n	Means (95% CI)	n	Means (95% CI)
Baseline				
8				
12				
16				
24				
36				
48				

Change in HbA1c from Baseline to Week 48 or Last HabA1c Measured prior to Rescue Therapy

- We will report and evaluate the number who received rescue therapy by treatment arm.
- The mean difference in the change from baseline to week 48 HbA1c or last measurement prior to rescue therapy will be tested using a T-test.
- The assumptions of the T-test will be assessed.
  - Quintile-Quintile plots will be used to assess normality.
  - An F-test will be used to test for equal variances between the two treatment groups. If the variances are unequal, we will use Welch's test.

Change in Measurements

- We will use a repeated measures mixed model to test whether athelis changes measurements over time.
- Fixed effects include treatment group, baseline measurement, and study time.
- Plots of change over study time will be constructed for each measurement and treatment group.

The table below shows the measurements of interest.

Table 12.5 Change in Measurements from Baseline by Treatment Group

Measurement	Treatment Group	Mean Delta (95% Confidence Limits)	P val*	Mean Difference Between Treatment Groups** (95% Confidence Limits)	P val*
Weight, kg	Placebo				
	3.5 g				
Glucose, mg/dl	Placebo				
	3.5 g				
Cholesterol, mg/dl	Placebo				
	3.5 g				
HDL, mg/dl	Placebo				
	3.5 g				
LDL (direct), md/dl	Placebo				
	3.5 g				
Log Triglyceride, mg/dl***	Placebo				
	3.5 g				
Cholesterol/HDL	Placebo				
	3.5 g				
LDL/HDL	Placebo				
	3.5 g				

Measurement	Treatment Group	Mean Delta (95% Confidence Limits)	P val*	Mean Difference Between Treatment Groups** (95% Confidence Limits)	P val*

*Ho: μ=0

**3.5 minus Placebo

***Back Transformed

Index

A

Adolescent Medicine Trials Network (ATN) for HIV/AIDS Intervention 11
aims 22, 23
analysis
  about 59
  general approach to 60
  of questions/hypotheses 19, 63, 83
  sensitivity 69
  subgroup 69
  unplanned 75
analysis plan example 78
analysis policy
  about 6
  components of 7
  example project 11
  for large projects 11
  for TIAD study 82
ANOVA procedure 60

B

baseline tables
  for TIAD study 80
  producing 55
BY processing 74

C

cases 30
Chi-square test 80
co-investigator, responsibilities for 25
COLLINOINT option 68
communicating, importance of 73
conclusions, potential 71
confounding variables
  about 67
  identifying 31
CONTENTS procedure 35
Cook's D plot 53
covariates 67
cross-references 75

D

data
  reading 34
  reviewing with study team 37
data analysis plans
  about 3
  as a component of analysis policies 8
  types of 3
data analysis proposals, as a component of analysis policies 8
data collection roles 25
data definitions 35
data description
  about 33
  as a typical plan component 18
  data definitions 35
  data in hand 34
  data not in hand 33
  data sources 33
  data summary 36
  for TIAD study 79
  reading data 34
  reviewing data with study team 37
data exploration
  about 39
  as a typical plan component 18

communicating with project team 57
descriptive statistics for major variables 40
determining source of variability 49
distribution problems 46
outliers 42
problematic distributions 42
producing baseline tables 55
data in hand 34
data not in hand 33
data policies, as a component of analysis policies 8
data preparation and processing roles 25
data sources 33
data summary 36
data tables, for TIAD study 80
descriptive statistics, for major variables 40
detailed analysis plan 3
distribution problems 46

E

editor, responsibilities for 25
example project, analysis policy 11
experimental studies 29

F

Fisher's exact test 80
FREQ procedure 36, 41, 55

G

Gantt chart 72
GANTT procedure 72
general statistical approach
  as a typical plan component 18
  for TIAD study 82
GLIMMIX procedure 63
GLM procedure 52, 60

GROUPMEANS option 65

H

HbA1c response, for TIAD study 83
HOLM option 61
HOVTEST option 51
hypotheses/questions
  about 22, 23, 27, 29
  analysis of 63, 83
  as a typical plan component 18
  conceptualizing the problem 28
  for TIAD study 79
  primary 63
  research 29
  secondary 69

I

illustrator, responsibilities for 25
inclusion 30
intention to treat (ITT) analyses 10, 79, 83
Internal Review Board (IRB) 9
introduction
  about 21
  aims 22, 23
  as a typical plan component 18, 21
  hypotheses 22
  objectives 22
  questions 22, 23

J

junior statistician, responsibilities for 25

L

large projects, analysis policy for 11

lead statistician/analyst, responsibilities for 25
limitations, of studies 72
longitudinal data analysis, for TIAD study 82

M

mean 48
MEANS procedure 36, 40, 55, 62
MEANS statement 50, 51
median 48
MI procedure 63
missing values 62
mission statement, as a component of analysis policies 7
MIXED procedure 63
MULTTEST procedure 60

N

National Institute of Child Health and Human Development (NICHD) 11
NMISS option, MEANS procedure 62
NORMAL option 43
NPERG= option 65
Nurses Health Study 11

O

objectives 22
observational studies 29
ODS statement 74
outable= option 36
outcomes
  for TIAD study 79
  specifying 31
outliers, exploring 42
Output Delivery System (ODS) 36, 74

P

parameters, statistical 60
plans
  about 17
  outline of 18
  revising 73
  turning into reports 74
plot=diagnostics option, GLM procedure 52
potential conclusions
  about 71
  as a typical plan component 19
power 64
POWER procedure 64
primary hypotheses 63
primary outcomes
  about 31
  for TIAD study 79
principal investigator, responsibilities for 25
PRINT procedure 55
problematic distributions, exploring 42
problems, conceptualizing 28
programmer, responsibilities for 25
project director, responsibilities for 25
project initiation, as a component of analysis policies 7
project team
  communicating with 57
  identifying 24
  roles and responsibilities for 25
proposal analysis plan 3

Q

quantile-quantile (Q-Q) plot 48
quasi-experimental study 30
questions/hypotheses
  about 22, 23, 27, 29
  analysis of 63, 83
  as a typical plan component 18
  conceptualizing the problem 28
  for TIAD study 79

primary 63
research 29
secondary 69

SUMMARY procedure 36, 40

R

randomized controlled trial (RCT) 30
REG procedure 68
REPORT procedure 36, 40, 55
reporting guidelines, as a component of analysis policies 10
reports, turning plans into 74
research questions 29
revising the plan 73
rich text format (RTF) 36

T

t-test 80
tabular presentations, developing 74
TABULATE procedure 40, 55, 74
target audience, identifying 25
templates 72, 81
TIAD study example 78
timeline
  about 72
  as a typical plan component 19
TWOSAMPLEMEANS statement 65

S

sample size 64
secondary hypotheses 69
secondary outcomes
  about 31
  for TIAD study 79
sensitivity analysis 69
SHEET_INTERVAL option 74
skewness 48
SQL procedure 36
SQUARE option 43
statistical parameters 60
statistical policies, as a component of analysis policies 9
studies
  limitations of 72
  timeline for 72
  types of 29
  weaknesses of 72
study team
  communicating with the 32
  for TIAD study 78
  reviewing data with 37
subgroup analyses 31, 69

U

UNIVARIATE procedure 36, 42, 46
unplanned analysis 75

V

values, missing 62
variability, determining source of 49
variable distributions, for TIAD study 80
variables
  confounding 31, 67
  descriptive statistics for major 40

W

weaknesses
  as a typical plan component 19
  of studies 72
WELCH option 51
Wilcoxon rank sum test 80

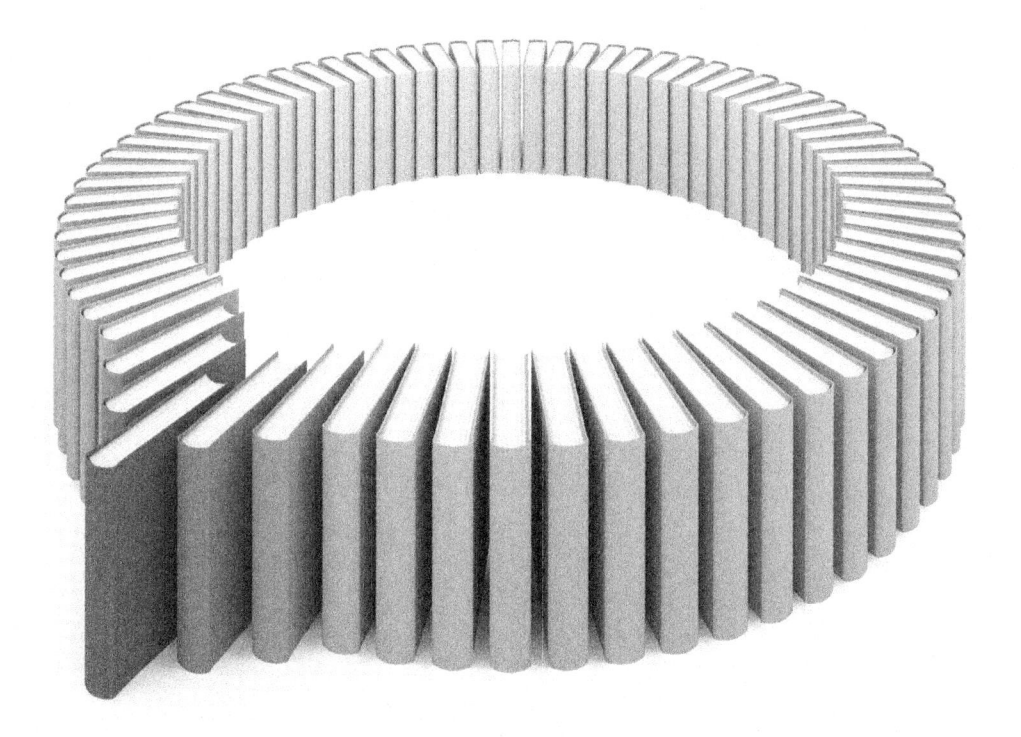

Gain Greater Insight into Your SAS® Software with SAS Books.

Discover all that you need on your journey to knowledge and empowerment.

support.sas.com/bookstore
for additional books and resources.

§.sas.
THE POWER TO KNOW.

SAS and all other SAS Institute Inc. product or service names are registered trademarks or trademarks of SAS Institute Inc. in the USA and other countries. ® indicates USA registration. Other brand and product names are trademarks of their respective companies. © 2013 SAS Institute Inc. All rights reserved. S107969US.0413

CPSIA information can be obtained at www.ICGtesting.com
Printed in the USA
BVOW09s1243230916

462929BV00010B/14/P

9 781629 604459